MANUEL CERRATO

From Dream to Spotlight

A Step-by-Step Guide to Turning Awards into Success Stories for Personal and Business Growth.

Copyright © 2024 by Manuel Cerrato

All rights reserved. No part of this publication may be reproduced, stored or transmitted in any form or by any means, electronic, mechanical, photocopying, recording, scanning, or otherwise without written permission from the publisher. It is illegal to copy this book, post it to a website, or distribute it by any other means without permission.

First edition

This book was professionally typeset on Reedsy. Find out more at reedsy.com

Contents

Preface	v
1 Introduction	1
2 Understanding the Value of Awards	5
Exploration of Industry-Specific Awards	7
Benefits of Recognition in Professional Settings	11
Aligning Awards with Career Milestones	14
Final Insights	17
3 Crafting a Compelling Award Application	19
Identifying Key Strengths and Achievements	20
Tailoring Applications for Specific Awards	22
Using Storytelling to augment Your Narrative	25
Insights and Implications	28
4 Overcoming Self-Doubt	29
Recognizing and Addressing Imposter Syndrome	30
Mindfulness and Self-Care Practices	33
Setting Realistic and Attainable Goals	35
Bringing It All Together	38
5 Building Your Personal Brand Through Awards	39
Defining Your Unique Selling Proposition	40
Aligning Brand Image with Award Criteria	43
Leveraging Media Exposure Post-Award	45
Summary and Reflections	48
6 Networking to Enhance Award Opportunities	50
Connecting with Past Winners and Jurors	51

Utilizing Social Media to Share Successes	54
Attending Industry Events for Exposure	56
Insights and Implications	59
7 Emotional Resilience and Professional Growth	60
Developing Coping Strategies for Rejection	61
Maintaining Motivation Through Adversity	64
Incorporating Stress-Reduction Techniques	66
Concluding Thoughts	68
8 Transformative Power of Recognition	70
Increasing Motivation Through Achievement	71
Shaping Company Culture with Recognition	74
Paving the Way for Future Opportunities	76
Final Insights	79
9 Leveraging Award Wins for Business Growth	81
Integrating Awards into Marketing Strategies	82
Expanding Reach through Public Relations	84
Attracting Clients and Investors Using Awards	87
Wrapping Up	90
10 Strategic Follow-Up After Winning Awards	92
Creating a Post-Award Action Plan	93
Tracking Metrics for Long-Term Impact	95
Engaging with Award Sponsors and Judges	98
Lessons Learned	101
11 Continuous Growth Beyond Awards	102
Evaluating Past Performances for Insights	103
Exploring New Areas for Development	105
Staying Updated on Industry Trends	108
Final Thoughts	112
12 Conclusion	113
References	117

Preface

Writing this book is, in many ways, a continuation of my own journey—a journey shaped by failures, perseverance, outstanding achievements, and an unwavering belief in the power of dreaming big. My own path has been defined by failures—four universities and an aviation school, each representing a dream I couldn't quite reach. It was only after these setbacks that I found my footing through an athletic scholarship, a pathway that later took me to graduate school in Europe. There, I turned my thesis into a startup, one that would go on to win both national and international recognition.

These awards opened doors I never imagined: consulting opportunities, executive positions, and large-scale projects where I managed millions of dollars. The irony? Each step toward these achievements began with failure. I've since gone from being a struggling student to becoming an aerospace engineer, an award-winning entrepreneur, a government official, a successful consultant, and now, full circle, back in my role as an entrepreneur, mentor, and coach under the guidance of John Maxwell through Maxwell Leadership. Along the way, I've experienced firsthand how transformative it can be to set audacious goals, pursue them with passion, and embrace every opportunity for growth.

The idea behind this book is simple: to show you that the path to success is rarely a straight line. It's filled with detours, challenges, and moments of doubt. But through it all, I want to encourage you to keep dreaming, to keep striving, and to view awards not just as recognition, but as powerful tools—tools that can open doors, build credibility, and connect you with like-minded people who share your vision.

I wish I had kept track of every award, grant, certificate, and trophy I've received over the years. Many were lost during moves from one city to another, or even from one country to another. Yet the memories and experiences remain vividly alive in my mind and heart. These accolades were not just milestones; they were stepping stones that reminded me of what's possible when we push ourselves beyond limits.

I wrote this book because I believe anyone—no matter where they start—has the potential to achieve extraordinary results. If I can do it, so can you. My hope is that the strategies, insights, and stories in these pages will inspire you to pursue your own dreams, set bold goals, and realize that the recognition you deserve is within your reach.

I invite you to dream big, act with purpose, and harness the power of awards to elevate your journey—just as I have. Let this book be your guide to taking that first step toward the success you've always envisioned. And if I can help you along the way, please don't hesitate to reach out. The best place to connect with me is on LinkedIn: linkedin.com/in/manucerrato.

1

Introduction

Have you ever thought about how a single distinction could not only validate your efforts but also propel your career to new heights? Imagine receiving an award that opens doors you never thought possible. Awards go beyond being just polished trophies or printed certificates; they're gateways to newfound opportunities and a way to cement your reputation in your field. Whether you're just starting in your profession or already a seasoned business veteran, recognition can transform your journey.

Let me take you back to a moment in my life that changed everything. I vividly remember standing at my first major award ceremony, the warmth of the spotlight on my face and the electric buzz of anticipation filling the room. As my company's name echoed through the room, followed by my own, I walked up to receive the award, my heart pounding with a mix of excitement and disbelief. The audience's applause felt like an endorsement of every late night, every setback overcome, and every risk taken. At that moment, my understanding of personal worth and professional potential was completely reshaped. An award can be more than just an honor; it can ignite a fire within you, fueling a passion that pushes you to reach further than you ever imagined.

This book is designed to guide you through the rewarding yet often misunderstood world of awards and recognition. The strategies outlined here will provide pathways to gain credibility and visibility for young professionals and aspiring entrepreneurs keen on establishing their brands. And for those who are established in their careers, looking to refresh their brand reputation and enhance their authority, you'll find insights on leveraging strategic award participation to secure your place as a leader in your industry. Throughout these pages, we will explore practical steps and strategies that demystify the award application process and foster personal growth. Recognition shouldn't just be seen as a flourish on your resume; it's a launchpad for transformation.

Many people hesitate when considering applying for awards, burdened by self-doubt and a fear of rejection. This is perfectly normal—it's human nature to wonder if you're genuinely deserving or if you even stand a chance in the competition. You might worry about appearing overconfident or fear the sting of hearing "no." But what if I told you that each award application is not just a gamble but a valuable opportunity for growth, regardless of the outcome? Every step you take towards recognition builds resilience and sharpens your skills. It transforms challenges into lessons and failures into stepping stones towards success.

INTRODUCTION

Awards have the unique ability to influence how others perceive us and how we perceive ourselves. They can amplify your voice in a crowded marketplace and position you as a thought leader in your domain. Consider this book your roadmap to unlocking that potential. We'll dive into choosing the right awards to pursue, crafting compelling applications, and preparing yourself to step into the limelight with confidence. Alongside tactical advice, you'll find stories of individuals who, through awards, experienced breakthroughs they never anticipated, proving the limitless possibilities that recognition can bring.

As you embark on this quest, think of it not just as chasing awards but embracing the process of putting yourself out there and acknowledging your accomplishments. It's about building the courage to say, "I am worthy of recognition," and taking deliberate action towards making that statement a reality. Together, we'll tackle insecurities and inseminate the mindset that these accolades are within your reach, amplifying your impact and broadening your horizons.

You'll learn how to approach awards with a strategic mindset through relatable anecdotes, expert tips, and real-world case studies. You won't just apply; you'll compete with purpose. It's time to start seeing awards not as distant dreams but as tangible goals that, when achieved, can revolutionize your career and shape your professional narrative.

Picture yourself finally being recognized for your hard work, pictured in articles, invited to speak at conferences, and respected by peers and mentors alike. Award-winning status isn't reserved for an elite few—it's accessible to you with the proper preparation and mindset. With the knowledge you'll gain from this book, you'll be well-equipped to make informed decisions, spot opportunities, and craft a compelling story that stands out amongst the crowd.

This is not only about winning awards—it's about becoming the best you can be while trying to achieve them. Each chapter builds upon a foundation of empowerment and education, ensuring that by the end of this book, you'll be ready to step confidently into the arena of recognition.

Welcome to an adventure where acknowledgment awaits, aligning with your aspirations and pushing you towards achievements once thought impossible. Allow this book to illuminate your path, encouraging you to seize the accolades that have always been within your grasp. Let's start redefining what awards mean to you and transforming how they can impact your professional life.

2

Understanding the Value of Awards

Have you ever wondered why some individuals and organizations soar above the rest, garnering recognition and accolades along their journey? Awards are potent tools that can significantly elevate careers and improve reputations. Research shows that award-winning companies experience increased customer trust, improved employee morale, and improved financial performance.

Understanding how awards impact individuals and businesses can be transformative in our fast-paced world. They help set benchmarks, inspire innovation, and foster connections that might not otherwise emerge. As we navigate the terrain of career advancement and enterprise development, awards become tools for aligning efforts with broader goals. By participating in award programs, professionals gain recognition, which often opens doors to new opportunities, whether it be through heightened visibility or enhanced credibility within an industry.

Achieving both local and international awards has profoundly influenced my professional trajectory. This recognition garnered substantial media coverage, enhancing my visibility and unlocking numerous opportunities. I secured contracts worth over six figures, demonstrating the significant financial rewards that recognition can bring. Each project enriched my portfolio and reinforced my standing in the industry. As I dedicated myself to these initiatives, the results underscored my expertise, inspiring me to strive for excellence in all my pursuits.

As an entrepreneur and consultant, I delivered services that empowered businesses, international organizations, and research institutions to execute projects and enhance outcomes in their regions. These organizations sought my guidance, attracted by my honors and proven success stories. This engagement allowed me to demonstrate my abilities in diverse settings, broadening my influence and forging meaningful connections with other professionals. Numerous full-time job offers came my way, each promising new challenges and opportunities for growth. However, at the start of my professional career, I chose to focus on my own projects, prioritizing my entrepreneurial vision over traditional career paths.

The attention from various governments, NGOs, and universities resulted in visits to our facilities. Their interest validated that the awards were not just ceremonial; They generated concrete outcomes that advanced our initiatives.

Interactions with these visiting groups led to invaluable insights and networking prospects. I recounted my experiences, illustrating how the recognition from the awards influenced my strategies and aspirations. Many expressed a keen interest in forming partnerships, highlighting the profound ripple effect that accolades can generate. By nurturing these connections, I promoted my work and encouraged collaboration across different sectors, fostering a culture of knowledge and resource-sharing. Each encounter reinforced the belief that these awards celebrated not just individual achievements; They paved the way for collective growth and advancement throughout the community.

Exploration of Industry-Specific Awards

To fully harness the potential of recognition, it's essential to understand the various types of awards across industries and how they align with one's career or business goals.

Awards come in many forms, from local acknowledgments to prestigious global honors. Local awards often focus on community impact and help individuals or businesses establish their reputation within their immediate environment. For example, regional chambers of commerce may offer annual awards recognizing businesses contributing to local economic growth. Such awards are necessary to build grassroots connections, promote community goodwill, and enhance regional stakeholders' visibility.

On a national level, awards often emphasize broader contributions, such as industry innovation or outstanding performance across multiple regions. For instance, the Malcolm Baldrige National Quality Award in the U.S. recognizes organizations demonstrating excellence in leadership, strategy, and customer engagement (Eastman, 2010). Being recognized at this level elevates the recipient's standing in the industry and offers a competitive edge by showcasing its commitment to quality and improvement.

Global awards, meanwhile, represent the pinnacle of recognition, celebrating groundbreaking innovations and significant contributions that transcend borders. These awards spotlight the leaders in industry and technology, providing them with an international platform to influence peers and shape future trends. A global award signifies excellence, adaptability, and foresight in addressing worldwide challenges.

A prominent example in this category is the awards organized by XPrize, a non-profit organization that promotes global competitions designed to encourage technological and scientific innovations that tackle the greatest challenges facing humanity. Founded by Dr. Peter H. Diamandis, a visionary whose work has inspired countless innovators, XPrize redefines the boundaries of what humanity can achieve. From private space exploration to breakthroughs in clean energy, water access, and healthcare, Diamandis has demonstrated the power of bold thinking to address global challenges.

On a personal level, I've always felt a curious sense of alignment with Dr. Diamandis's mission. Like him, I began my career in aerospace engineering, drawn by a desire to explore the frontiers of what's possible. Over the years, I've had the privilege of working on large-scale projects addressing clean energy, water solutions, and public health—fields where our paths and passions seem to intersect. Perhaps it's serendipity, or perhaps it's the universal pull of shared ideals that connect those of us driven by a desire to create meaningful impact.

His work has been a beacon for me, lighting the way as I chart my own course in pursuit of ambitious goals. Through his books, such as *Abundance* and *Bold,* and the bold initiatives of XPrize, I've found not only inspiration but also affirmation that dreaming big and taking decisive action are essential ingredients for transformative change.

For me, this connection reinforces a powerful truth: the world needs dreamers and doers—people who dare to think differently, tackle audacious challenges, and believe that the impossible is within reach. Whether through XPrize, personal endeavors, or global awards, we all have the potential to shape the future. And perhaps, along the way, we'll discover that those we admire most are not just mentors but kindred spirits, reminding us that our dreams are part of a much greater tapestry of human achievement.

Understanding different awards' criteria and focus areas is fundamental for crafting effective application strategies. Many awards target specific sectors or themes, such as technological innovation, sustainability, or social impact. Examining these criteria allows applicants to tailor their submissions to highlight relevant achievements and innovative approaches. For instance, awards like the Digital Innovation of the Year honor those making strides in integrating technology into learning environments (News, 2024). Applicants need to show their technical skills and the real benefits these have had on education.

Emerging awards have gained traction in response to evolving industries and societal needs. These newer categories reflect the dynamic nature of modern industries and provide recognition in areas such as digital transformation, diversity, and sustainability. As industries change rapidly, new awards are introduced to acknowledge efforts in addressing contemporary challenges. For example, the Excellence in Data and Insight award celebrates advancements in data management and analytics, showcasing how real-time insights drive efficiency and improve decision-making (News, 2024).

The rise of such awards illustrates the growing emphasis on forward-thinking initiatives and encourages professionals to embrace innovative strategies. Engaging with these emerging awards provides recognition across cutting-edge fields and enables networking opportunities with other innovators and thought leaders. By participating actively, individuals and organizations can position themselves as pioneers within their sectors, attracting partnerships and collaborations that can lead to further development and success.

Engaging with awards can bolster the brand and visibility of young professionals and entrepreneurs in their fields. Awards offer validation and serve as testimonials to one's competence and expertise. By strategically selecting awards that align with their goals, professionals can improve their resumes and profiles, making them more attractive to potential employers, clients, or partners. Aspiring entrepreneurs can use awards as leverage when seeking investments or collaborations, turning recognition into tangible business advantages.

On the other hand, established business owners can use awards to refresh their brand image and assert their authority in the industry. Awards provide an opportunity to showcase sustained excellence and adaptiveness to market changes. Participating in reputable recognition programs can reinvigorate a brand's public perception, signaling ongoing relevance and dedication to high standards.

Benefits of Recognition in Professional Settings

In today's fast-paced world, the importance of recognition in professional settings cannot be overstated. Whether one is an individual contributor or part of a dynamic organization, receiving awards can bring about numerous advantages that extend far beyond mere personal satisfaction. One of the most significant advantages is increased credibility. When individuals or organizations receive awards, it sends a powerful message to peers, clients, and stakeholders. An award can act as a testament to one's dedication, skill, and capability, often influential in decision-making processes.

Consider the scenario of a startup entering a competitive market. By building trust with potential clients, awards can help differentiate this newcomer from established competitors. The recognition gained through awards signals expertise and reliability that can ease clients' hesitation when choosing between similar service providers. This enhanced credibility applies to businesses and professionals, as securing honors can validate their skills and strengthen their reputation among colleagues and industry leaders—a reality I've experienced firsthand.

Awards magnify visibility in ways few other achievements can. Take, for instance, how prestigious awards can propel a company into the spotlight. Suddenly, the business is featured in media outlets or invited to participate in high-profile industry conferences, opening doors to new opportunities. For example, a tech company winning an innovation award might attract coverage from technology blogs and magazines, leading to increased interest from consumers and businesses seeking partnerships. This heightened visibility can cascade, generating referrals and networking prospects that were previously out of reach.

For individuals, increased visibility through awards can lead to similar perks. Professionals who earn industry recognition often find themselves subject to increased attention from recruiters and headhunters looking for top talent. Being publicly recognized for one's work can lead to speaking engagements, guest writing opportunities, or invitations to join prestigious panels or boards. These activities further establish one's presence and influence in their field, contributing to long-term career development.

Recognition plays a pivotal role in boosting motivation and morale among teams. When employees feel their hard work is acknowledged and celebrated, they are more likely to remain engaged and productive. This connection aligns with employee recognition theories, such as reinforcement theory and Maslow's hierarchy of needs, where positive acknowledgment encourages desirable behaviors and enables a sense of belonging. Studies show that recognition increases job satisfaction and reduces turnover rates, leading to improved team performance (Team, 2024).

Sometimes, you don't even need to apply for awards—someone else might nominate you without your knowledge. Your professional success or your company's performance can earn you a place in annual recognition ceremonies or industry events.

For example, while working for the United States Agency for International Development (USAID) in El Salvador, I had the humbling honor of being part of a team that received the Superior Honor Group Award. This prestigious agency-wide recognition celebrated our innovative approach, collaborative efforts, and exceptional problem-solving skills. The achievement culminated in the successful implementation of a $53 million multi-bank loan guarantee program in Central America. This award is just one of many I received during my time with USAID's regional office in Central America. Additionally, I was honored to serve as a judge and evaluator, assessing award nominations, often requesting additional information to ensure the most deserving candidates were recognized.

Creating an environment where awards and recognition are prioritized promotes positivity and encourages individuals to strive for excellence. Seeing their efforts validated through awards can instill a sense of pride and ownership in team members, reinforcing their commitment to organizational goals. For managers, fostering such an atmosphere can be invaluable in promoting collaboration and encouraging employees to go above and beyond.

Honors can serve as catalysts for cultural cohesion in organizations. When employees collectively work toward achieving recognition, it fosters unity and reinforces the shared values that define an organization's culture. Employees become more attuned to the core mission and values, directing their efforts to meet overarching corporate objectives. This harmony can significantly improve the workplace atmosphere, enhancing overall productivity and morale.

The narrative continues after immediate gains. Awards can have long-lasting impacts by acting as benchmarks for future growth and success. Organizations and individuals can use past honors as milestones, reflecting on them as progress indicators while striving for continued excellence. Such achievements encourage momentum, stimulate innovation, and inspire individuals to push boundaries to pursue more significant accomplishments.

Aligning Awards with Career Milestones

The process of career progression often feels like a winding path with milestones that mark significant achievements along the way. Among these milestones, recognitions stand out as strategic markers that validate past accomplishments and guide future ambitions. For young professionals and seasoned entrepreneurs alike, understanding how to map their career progression by leveraging awards can transform their brand in compelling ways.

Honors reflect both growth and transition. They tell a story about where you've been and signal where you're heading. Mapping career progression involves identifying points in your professional life where an award could reflect your development. This practice can help professionals align their long-term goals with these honors, allowing them to demonstrate their capabilities and growth to peers and industry leaders effectively. When charting a career path, consider how specific awards can highlight transitions or advancements, such as moving from an entry-level position to a management role. Each award becomes a testament to your evolving skill set and commitment to your field.

Awards act as tangible goal markers—stepping stones toward greater achievement. Setting specific milestones linked to pursuing distinctions can infuse one's career strategy with motivation and focus. Imagine each honor as a destination on your career roadmap; defining what you want to achieve before reaching each point can streamline your efforts and encourage perseverance through challenges. This approach encourages individuals to proactively set ambitious goals that meet award criteria, ultimately driving personal and professional excellence. For example, if an industry award emphasizes innovation, aspiring candidates might prioritize developing new initiatives or products in their organizations to showcase in future award cycles.

Having a long-term vision is essential when pursuing awards, as it ensures consistency with your ultimate career aspirations and legacy building. This vision requires looking beyond immediate recognition to understand how each award contributes to the grander scope of one's career goals. The process involves winning a prize and strategically selecting those that resonate with one's desired career trajectory. It's about curating a narrative around your successes, highlighting your contributions to your field, and preparing you for future opportunities.

As you craft this vision, consider the impact of each award on your professional legacy. What message does it send about your priorities and expertise? How does it bolster your credibility and influence in your industry? With a well-defined vision, awards can serve as more than mere acknowledgments—they become integral parts of your career blueprint, helping build a lasting reputation and inspiring others to follow your lead.

To maximize the impact of awards on your career, it's wise to develop strategies for tailoring achievements to fit specific honors. This involves understanding each award's unique attributes and expectations and shaping your accomplishments accordingly. Whether it's enhancing leadership qualities, advancing innovative projects, or expanding community service involvement, identifying areas for improvement can increase your chances of securing awards that resonate with your vision.

Incorporating honors into your career strategy isn't solely about personal gain. It's also about contributing positively to the culture and values of your organization and the industry at large. Awards can reinforce a sense of community and collective achievement, encouraging peers to aspire toward similar standards of excellence and cultivating a shared sense of purpose in teams.

Recognizing the intrinsic value of awards beyond the physical trophy is also essential. While external validation can inject confidence and enthusiasm into your professional pursuits, the journey toward achieving these accolades offers invaluable learning experiences and growth opportunities. From developing essential skills to expanding your professional network, engaging in award processes cultivates attributes that enrich personal fulfillment and career success.

Final Insights

This chapter explored the diverse landscape of awards and how they connect with personal ambitions and business goals. Whether you're just starting in your career or are an established professional, understanding the variety of awards available—from local to global—can significantly impact your career progression. By learning about their criteria and purposes, individuals can strategically pursue those that best match their objectives. Local awards might help build community reputation, national ones could highlight innovation and excellence, while international recognitions place you on the global stage as a leader in your field. Such distinctions validate achievements and open doors for new opportunities and connections.

For young professionals and entrepreneurs, engaging with awards is a way to boost visibility and craft a formidable personal brand. These acknowledgments are powerful testimonials of competence, making profiles more attractive to potential employers or partners. For seasoned professionals, awards offer a chance to reaffirm industry standing and inject renewed vigor into their brand image. New awards categories emerge as industries evolve, reflecting contemporary challenges and innovations. Embracing these changes encourages growth and adaptation, ensuring ongoing relevance. Ultimately, awards contribute to a rich narrative of success, guiding future endeavors and enhancing one's legacy in the professional world.

As we wrap up this chapter, the upcoming section will unveil powerful strategies for crafting noteworthy submissions. We will examine the critical elements of a successful application, covering everything from conducting a personal SWOT analysis to developing a narrative that genuinely connects. Get ready to discover actionable insights that will convert your accomplishments into an outstanding submission. But what are the key secrets that can raise your application beyond the ordinary?

3

Crafting a Compelling Award Application

D id you know that a well-crafted award application can be the key to unlocking career-changing opportunities? Yet, according to industry reports, many deserving professionals and businesses miss out on awards simply because their applications fail to stand out.

Crafting a compelling award application is an art that blends self-reflection, storytelling, and strategic presentation. In the competitive world of professional recognition, knowing how to present one's strengths and achievements can make all the difference. As individuals seek to highlight their unique qualities and significant contributions, capturing the essence of what makes them stand out becomes important. It's about weaving together experiences in such a way that they not only meet the criteria but also resonate with judges, leaving a lasting impression.

Identifying Key Strengths and Achievements

When crafting a compelling award application, one of the most critical steps is recognizing and articulating your most notable strengths and achievements. This requires thoughtful reflection and organization to ensure your application captures the essence of what makes you and your work stand out. Here's how you can achieve this effectively.

Conducting a personal SWOT analysis (Strengths, Weaknesses, Opportunities, and Threats) is an excellent starting point for identifying strengths and opportunities that align with award criteria. This strategic tool helps you evaluate your internal attributes—your strengths and weaknesses—alongside external factors like opportunities and threats. Doing so lets you present a clear picture of where you excel, what challenges you face, and what external conditions you can leverage in your application. Start by listing your strengths—those qualities or skills that give you a competitive advantage. These might include leadership skills, technical proficiency, or unique experiences. For example, if you've received industry recognition or completed specialized training, these are standout details to highlight. Seeking advice from peers or mentors can offer fresh perspectives on strengths you may not have recognized. Feedback from others often uncovers hidden gems that can transform an average application into an outstanding one.

Opportunities are another critical component. Look beyond current roles to identify potential areas to capitalize on, such as upcoming projects or networking prospects that showcase your abilities. Think about any trends or initiatives within your industry where your strengths could shine. This forward-thinking approach strengthens your application and demonstrates your proactive engagement in your field. By regularly updating your SWOT analysis, you make sure your narrative stays relevant and compelling.

Creating an accomplishments inventory is another powerful technique for structuring your achievements. Begin by documenting your successes in detail, including key metrics and outcomes. This involves more than just listing your achievements; it's about painting a vivid picture of your professional journey. For instance, instead of simply noting that you led a project, explain how your leadership brought about a 20% increase in productivity or significantly increased team morale. Your goal is to convey the tangible impact of your contributions. An organized inventory is a rich resource, making it easy to adjust your applications to various awards by drawing upon a robust selection of achievements. Ensure this document is updated regularly to capture improvements and new accomplishments, as staying current adds credibility and dynamism to your application.

Highlighting your unique skills is equally important. In award applications, hard and soft skills are vital as they reflect your ability to deliver results. Soft skills such as communication, teamwork, and problem-solving should be illustrated through real-world examples demonstrating their impact. For instance, if you successfully negotiated a partnership that opened new revenue streams, detail how your communication and negotiation skills were pivotal. This narrative approach helps reviewers visualize your contributions and understand the breadth of your skill set. Framing your skills in terms of their impact ensures they resonate more profoundly with those reviewing your application.

As you build your application, weave together your SWOT insights, achievements inventory, and skill highlights into a coherent story that underscores your qualifications. Developing this narrative requires finesse; it's not just about stating facts but also storytelling. Relate your experiences to the award criteria, ensuring each element aligns with the goals and values of the recognition. For example, if an award emphasizes innovation, focus on moments when your creative solutions led to breakthroughs or efficiencies. Ensure every part of your application supports this central theme, creating a solid and cohesive message.

Tailoring Applications for Specific Awards

Adapting an award application to fulfill the distinct criteria and expectations of various awards resembles creating a customized recipe. Each ingredient, technique, and adjustment must be precisely calibrated to highlight and present the applicant's strengths most favorably. Just as no two recipes are alike, no two applications should be. Each award possesses unique characteristics, and acknowledging this can significantly enhance the likelihood of success.

The process starts with comprehensive research into the

award's requirements. While it may seem laborious, this groundwork is essential for crafting a persuasive application. Investigate the backgrounds of previous recipients—what qualities did they demonstrate? What unique elements made their submissions notable? This investigative work provides crucial insights into what the judges prioritize. Understanding the evaluation criteria is equally critical. Numerous organizations offer guidelines that outline explicit expectations for applicants. By tailoring your submission to these standards, you fulfill the necessary conditions and showcase your diligent preparation. Demonstrating an understanding of the award's significance places you in a favorable position from the outset.

Once equipped with insights from your research, the next phase is to adapt the language and tone of your application. Picture each award as possessing its own flavor. Awards focusing on innovation may be best expressed with dynamic and visionary language, while those recognizing community involvement might value empathy and warmth. To strike the right chord, pinpoint the primary values of the award—do they emphasize creativity, leadership, or environmental responsibility? Utilizing language that resonates with these values creates a bridge between the application and the judges, transforming it from a mere recitation of facts into a compelling narrative that aligns with the award's mission.

Showcasing relevant experiences is crucial in persuading the judges that you merit the award. Not every achievement or skill will correspond with the award's themes, so it is important to emphasize experiences closely related to the award's focus. Think of it as assembling a highlight reel; concentrate on pivotal moments that directly relate to the award's values. Utilize bullet points to present these experiences succinctly and effectively, ensuring they capture attention and stand out. This approach turns your application into a curated showcase of achievements that reflect the award's objectives.

The experience of creating a successful application is iterative. It involves more than producing a single draft and hoping for the best; it requires an ongoing refinement process. Begin by critically assessing your initial draft, questioning whether it adheres to the researched criteria and if the language resonates with the award's core values. Involve others in this process; feedback from colleagues, mentors, or previous award recipients can offer invaluable insights. Establish deadlines for these reviews, treating each round as a chance to polish and enhance your submission. The application becomes more refined and focused with every iteration, increasing the chances of captivating the judges' attention.

However, remember that meticulous customization and enhancement demand time and perseverance. Hurrying through steps or overlooking key elements may result in an application that, while complete, needs more depth and connection. Approach this process like crafting a rich narrative; each section requires time to develop fully before proceeding to the next.

Employing these strategies elevates the quality of your application and reflects your dedication and commitment to the endeavor. It demonstrates that you respect the award enough to invest substantial effort into producing a submission authentically representing your distinctive qualities and the award's values.

Using Storytelling to augment Your Narrative

One of the most effective strategies in crafting a compelling award application involves leveraging storytelling techniques to engage reviewers and highlight accomplishments. Storytelling does more than recount events; it creates connections and evokes emotions, making your achievements memorable and relatable. Consider employing a 'past, present, future' framework to create an engaging narrative that stands out. This approach helps to weave a story that highlights your achievements and provides a vision for where you aim to be.

The 'past, present, future' structure begins with reflecting on past experiences. Start by identifying significant milestones or breakthroughs in your path. These are experiences that have shaped who you are today. For instance, if you're applying for an innovation award, describe how an early fascination with technology led you to uncover solutions to existing problems. This sets the stage for reviewers to understand your motivations and initial steps toward success.

Moving into the present, this is where you will discuss your current accomplishments. Showcase your projects, skills, and attributes that match the award's criteria, emphasizing their significance. The key here is specificity—use concrete examples to illustrate what you've achieved and how it's impacted your field. But don't stop there; infuse your narrative with personal anecdotes that reveal your personality and drive. Perhaps a recent challenge pushed you to innovate, demonstrating resilience and creativity. By sharing these stories, you highlight your accomplishments and connect with the reviewers on a human level.

Looking towards the future, express your aspirations and how winning this award supports your goals. This aspect is crucial as it shows ambition and a commitment to continuous growth. Whether it's advancing in your career, developing new technologies, or inspiring others, articulate a clear vision of how the award will propel you forward. In doing so, you paint a picture of potential progress that adds depth to your narrative, inviting reviewers to invest in your continued path.

Conflict and resolution are essential elements of storytelling. Incorporate instances where you faced challenges and overcame them. These moments of adversity not only add drama to your story but also showcase resilience and problem-solving skills. Discuss the obstacles encountered and the lessons learned along the way. Perhaps you had to navigate a market downturn or adapt to unexpected changes in your industry. How did you rise above these obstacles? Highlighting these scenarios can powerfully communicate your perseverance and adaptability, traits highly valued in any professional setting.

To further humanize your application, share personal motivations and interactions that inspire you. Consider discussing mentors who guided you, teams that supported you, or pivotal interactions that influenced your career path. These elements contribute to a fuller picture of what you've accomplished and why those accomplishments matter to you personally. This human element can differentiate your application by making it relatable and genuine.

In addition to crafting a compelling written narrative, visual storytelling can strengthen your application. Visual aids such as timelines or infographics can successfully illustrate your journey, providing a concise summary of your achievements and contributions. Timelines can show progression over time, highlighting key moments that led to your success. Infographics can simplify complex data, making it easier for reviewers to grasp your impact at a glance. These visual tools complement your story, providing a holistic view of your accomplishments.

When leveraging visualizations, ensure they are relevant and well-designed. A cluttered or confusing infographic could detract from your narrative rather than improve it. Choose visuals that best represent your story and reflect the award's focus. For example, if showcasing technological advancements, a timeline detailing various stages of development might be particularly impactful.

Through this blend of narrative and visualization, your application becomes not only more engaging but also more persuasive. This multifaceted approach demonstrates your ability to communicate complex ideas clearly and creatively, a valuable skill in any field.

Insights and Implications

This chapter discussed how to tailor applications for specific awards, comparing it to making a custom suit. By looking into the award's criteria and previous winners, you can adjust your application to meet the judges' expectations. Using storytelling methods like the 'past, present, future' approach helps make your story more engaging. Adding elements like problem-solving and visual details make your application stand out. These strategies improve your submission, show dedication, and align your goals with the award's values. With this knowledge, you can create robust applications that showcase your achievements and commitment to growth and excellence in your field.

In the next chapter, we'll dive deeper into the feelings of self-doubt. We'll discuss practical strategies to counteract these challenges and empower you to present your best self in your applications. Overcoming self-doubt isn't just about boosting confidence; it's about embracing who you are at your core, despite the possible insecurities. What techniques will help you silence that inner critic? What steps will you take to reinforce your belief in yourself? The answers strengthen your application and transform your mindset entirely.

4

Overcoming Self-Doubt

Overcoming self-doubt is often a path filled with obstacles and opportunities for growth. It's that constant fear of not being enough or the nagging thought, "Do I really deserve this?" Many have felt its grip while striving to enhance their careers and achieve recognition. Whether you're applying for awards or simply trying to carve out your niche, self-doubt can act as both a motivator and a barrier.

This internal struggle is common among professionals and creatives alike, often surfacing when faced with new challenges or competitive environments. Research indicates that self-doubt is particularly prevalent among high achievers, with many experiencing what is known as impostor syndrome, where they doubt their accomplishments and fear being exposed as frauds.

Despite its universal presence, self-doubt is not an insurmountable foe. In fact, those who learn to navigate these choppy emotional waters often find themselves emerging on the other side stronger and more self-assured. Strategies such as self-reflection, goal setting, and seeking support from mentors can significantly mitigate the effects of self-doubt. By embracing the challenges that come with self-doubt, individuals can foster resilience and ultimately improve their personal and professional experiences. Recognizing that self-doubt is a natural part of growth can empower you to take bold steps toward your aspirations, transforming what once felt like a hindrance into a catalyst for success.

Recognizing and Addressing Imposter Syndrome

Imposter syndrome resonates with many, especially those striving for career recognition. It's the persistent sense of self-doubt coupled with the fear of being uncovered as a fraud, even in light of evident accomplishments. This phenomenon is surprisingly prevalent among high achievers. Psychologists Clance and Imes first coined the term in 1978, capturing these sentiments (Bravata et al., 2019). Today, it's recognized across diverse professional settings, highlighting its widespread impact on successful individuals.

Addressing impostor syndrome starts with understanding its triggers. Reflect on moments when self-doubt surfaced—high-pressure situations like applying for awards, asking for a raise, or meeting tight deadlines often spark these feelings. By analyzing past experiences, you can identify patterns in when and why self-doubt arises. Pinpointing these scenarios helps you mentally and emotionally prepare for future challenges, giving you the tools to confront impostor syndrome head-on.

Recognizing triggers aids in managing them effectively. For instance, if award applications make you question your worth, take a step back and review your accomplishments objectively. List your achievements, reminding yourself of the hard work and talent that led to success. This exercise can help break down the illusion of inadequacy.

Shifting one's mindset is another powerful approach to combating imposter syndrome. Cognitive-behavioral techniques can be instrumental here. They encourage reframing negative thoughts into positive affirmations. Start by identifying negative self-talk, such as "I don't deserve this award" or "I'm not good enough." Replace these thoughts with affirmations like "I have worked hard and earned this recognition" or "My skills are valuable." Over time, consistent practice of positive self-talk can gradually weaken the grip of self-doubt.

Visualizing success plays a vital role in building confidence. Picture yourself achieving goals and receiving accolades. This visualization promotes a sense of readiness, empowering you to face challenges head-on. It creates a mental blueprint for success, making it easier to manage stressful situations.

Building a support network also significantly helps overcome imposter syndrome. Engaging with peers, mentors, or relevant groups provides a platform for sharing experiences and receiving encouragement. Conversations with people who have faced similar struggles can create a sense of solidarity and normalcy, reinforcing the idea that self-doubt is a shared human experience.

Mentorship can be particularly beneficial for young professionals. Seeking guidance from someone more experienced offers valuable insights into managing career hurdles. A mentor can provide constructive feedback, helping you view your capabilities differently. Their stories of overcoming self-doubt can serve as motivation, showing that even the most accomplished individuals have faced insecurities.

Participating in networks or groups focused on professional development is equally essential. These platforms offer opportunities to connect with like-minded individuals, exchange knowledge, and celebrate each other's successes. Active involvement in such communities can boost confidence and lessen feelings of isolation.

It's important to understand that openly discussing these feelings reduces their power. When you express self-doubts, others can provide validation and perspective, emphasizing that you're not alone in these experiences. Sharing vulnerabilities fosters a supportive environment where growth and learning thrive.

Embracing your accomplishments is another step toward defeating imposter syndrome. Celebrating small victories is critical; each achievement contributes to overall progress, no matter how minor. Keeping a journal where you regularly note these wins reinforces a positive narrative around your abilities. Reflecting on your experience allows you to see the progression of your skills and talents over time.

Finally, practicing gratitude can shift focus from perceived shortcomings to actual strengths. Regularly acknowledging what you have achieved cultivates an abundance mindset. Gratitude exercises, such as writing thank-you notes to people who've contributed to your success, further reinforce this practice. This approach heightens self-awareness and encourages a positive outlook on your professional career.

Mindfulness and Self-Care Practices

Navigating the award application path can often stir up a well of self-doubt. Feelings of fear or failure often surface when striving for recognition in any domain. To combat this, cultivating mental resilience through mindfulness and self-care is essential—not only to stay grounded throughout the process but also to unlock your full potential as you pursue awards that can transform your personal brand and business.

Mindfulness, in particular, helps anchor you in the present moment, making it a potent antidote to the swirling thoughts of doubt and insecurity that can arise when you're preparing to submit an award application or meet a competitive deadline. Practices like meditation and breathing exercises can be powerful tools to quiet the inner critic, enabling you to approach the award process with greater clarity and focus.

For instance, when you're questioning your worth or the value of your achievements while preparing an award submission, taking a few mindful moments—like deep breathing or a brief meditation—can help redirect attention from negative thoughts to the steady rhythm of your breath. This simple act promotes calm and allows you to reconnect with your true strengths. These moments of clarity can lead to more robust, more confident presentations of your accomplishments, which are vital when competing for recognition.

Practicing mindfulness can help you better manage the stress often accompanying applying for awards. While you may be eager to gain recognition, the pressure to perform can easily lead to burnout. Incorporating mindfulness breaks and self-care routines into your daily life—whether through a quick outdoor walk, listening to music, or engaging in a hobby—allows you to reset mentally and physically. This helps you maintain your focus and productivity, ensuring you're at your best when presenting your work to judges or evaluators.

Creating a structured self-care routine with regular physical activity and balanced nutrition contributes to your overall mental well-being. By staying physically and mentally sharp, you position yourself for success not just in the short term but also in the long term. Winning awards and gaining recognition are as much about sustained effort as peak performance, and self-care enables you to maintain the endurance necessary to achieve those goals.

Regular reflection and gratitude practices can support personal growth by shifting your focus from perceived shortcomings to tangible accomplishments. Keeping a journal, for instance, where you reflect on your progress toward award submissions or other milestones can help you track your development and appreciate your progression. This not only boosts your confidence but also helps you present a stronger narrative when you apply for awards, transforming self-doubt into recognition of your ongoing achievements.

In short, mindfulness and self-care practices are necessary tools for anyone on the path to winning awards and gaining professional recognition. By nurturing your mental well-being, you build the resilience required to overcome self-doubt and present your true self with confidence. In doing so, you lay a solid foundation for personal transformation and business growth, enabling you to pursue your goals with clarity and assurance.

Setting Realistic and Attainable Goals

In the journey toward achieving recognition through awards, self-doubt can be a formidable hurdle. Often, the process of applying for awards feels overwhelming, which may lead professionals and entrepreneurs to question their abilities or second-guess their progress. One of the most effective ways to combat these feelings of uncertainty is by setting achievable goals that create a clear path forward and instill a sense of accomplishment. By using well-structured, realistic goals, you not only boost your morale but also ensure steady progress towards your objectives.

Adopting the SMART goals framework—which stands for Specific, Measurable, Achievable, Relevant, and Time-bound—can provide a structured method for setting goals in a way that reduces ambiguity and makes tracking progress more manageable. For example, when aiming to submit an award application, instead of vaguely targeting "improve my professional profile," a SMART goal might be: "Complete a detailed application draft for the [specific award name] within three weeks." This way, you can focus your energy on a tangible outcome and experience progress that motivates you to continue.

Breaking down significant objectives into smaller, more manageable tasks is another key element of this approach. Competing for awards can be daunting, but by dividing the larger goal—such as preparing an award submission—into smaller steps, like researching potential awards, gathering documentation, and writing each section of the application, you build momentum and maintain motivation. This method not only reduces stress but also provides consistent opportunities to celebrate small wins along the way, keeping you on track for the bigger prize.

This brings us to an important aspect of goal-setting: regularly reviewing and adjusting your goals. As professionals navigate the fast-paced and sometimes unpredictable landscape of award applications, it's important to be adaptable. Periodic reviews of your progress allow you to recalibrate your efforts, without spiraling into self-criticism if you encounter setbacks. For instance, if your initial goal to meet a submission deadline is challenged by unforeseen circumstances, extending the deadline or modifying the steps can ensure you remain focused on progress rather than perfection.

Another key tool in this process is leveraging accountability partners. These can be colleagues, mentors, or friends who understand your goals and can provide encouragement and feedback. When applying for industry awards, having someone who checks in on your progress and offers perspective can be invaluable. This network of support helps create a sense of shared purpose, making the process feel less solitary and more collaborative.

For young professionals eager to build their personal brand, these goal-setting strategies are especially powerful. As winning awards boosts credibility and visibility, aligning personal goals with award criteria becomes a strategic move toward career advancement. Established professionals, on the other hand, can use these techniques to make sure they remain relevant in their industry by targeting awards that reflect their evolving expertise and contributions.

By setting realistic, structured goals, breaking them down into actionable steps, and regularly reviewing your progress, you develop a strong foundation for success. Incorporating accountability partners along the way provides additional support and perspective, empowering you to overcome self-doubt and stay the course. Whether you're just beginning your professional career or are looking to refresh your approach, these practices equip you with the tools to manage the award application process with confidence and clarity—ultimately leading to both personal and professional growth.

Bringing It All Together

As we conclude this chapter, it becomes evident that managing self-doubt and cultivating confidence are critical components in your pursuit of awards. We've discussed how recognizing and addressing imposter syndrome allows you to confront those unsettling moments of self-doubt. Setting realistic goals through the SMART framework reinforces your path by providing a structured roadmap.

But how does this newfound confidence translate into tangible success? In the next chapter, we'll explore how awards do more than simply recognize your achievements—they are powerful tools for building and expanding your personal brand. By strategically leveraging your wins, you'll discover how to align your identity with the recognition you seek, gaining credibility and increased visibility and influence in your industry. We'll dive into actionable strategies like defining your unique selling proposition to strengthen your professional narrative and positioning yourself as a thought leader. How can you transform accolades into amplified industry presence and sustainable career growth? The answers await.

5

Building Your Personal Brand Through Awards

Imagine turning your achievements into powerful endorsements that define your industry presence. Awards are more than recognition—they're tools to elevate your personal brand and position you as a leader. Beyond showcasing success, they craft a narrative of resilience, expertise, and authenticity. But how can you transform recognition into lasting influence? This chapter explores how to strategically align your strengths, values, and achievements with the right opportunities to create a distinctive and compelling brand story.

By defining your unique selling proposition, aligning your brand image with award criteria, and leveraging media exposure post-award, you can maximize the impact of every recognition. Whether you're new to your field or a seasoned professional, the strategies in this chapter will help you establish thought leadership, build meaningful connections and unlock new opportunities.

Defining Your Unique Selling Proposition

As you embark on building your personal brand through awards, it's important to understand what sets you apart and how these accolades can mirror your unique strengths. In today's competitive landscape, standing out is more important than ever, and crafting a distinctive personal narrative is the first step in defining your brand identity.

Crafting your personal narrative involves weaving a story that effectively communicates your uniqueness and captures the essence of your professional career. This process requires introspection and creativity. Start by identifying significant milestones in your career—perhaps it's a project where you exceeded expectations or an initiative where your innovation led to success. These stories are about showcasing achievements and illustrating your growth, resilience, and the values that drive you. It's about creating a compelling tale that resonates with audiences and establishes you as a formidable presence in your field. By reflecting on these moments, you can highlight what makes you stand out and how you've overcome challenges, demonstrating your commitment and passion.

In conjunction with your narrative, identifying your core values becomes pivotal. Core values act as the guiding principles that define who you are and what you stand for. They shape your decisions and influence how others perceive you. When connecting these values with award categories, look for a match between what you represent and the purpose of the awards you're pursuing. For instance, if sustainability is a crucial value for you, seeking recognition in eco-friendly initiatives or leadership roles in green projects might be your path. Awards that reflect your values reinforce your brand and attract like-minded individuals and organizations, strengthening your professional network.

Showcasing expertise is vital in positioning yourself as a thought leader deserving of recognition. This goes beyond listing qualifications or past roles; it involves presenting your knowledge and skills in ways that demonstrate their impact and relevance. Consider participating in industry discussions, publishing articles, or speaking at conferences to share your insights and innovations. Each accolade you earn reinforces your credibility and highlights your contribution to your field. Awards endorse your expertise and indicate your readiness to lead and inspire others.

Building a personal brand statement ties all these elements together, briefly summarizing your brand promise. It's akin to a tagline—brief yet powerful enough to convey your message. When crafting this statement, focus on clarity and authenticity. It should encapsulate your experience, values, and what makes you unique. A well-constructed brand statement creates a memorable impression and becomes a cornerstone for all your marketing activities, including award applications. It signals to potential partners, employers, and collaborators precisely who you are and what you bring to the table.

To put these concepts into practice:

1. Begin by setting aside time to reflect on your career path.
2. Write down your significant experiences and consider

how they fit into a cohesive narrative.
3. Identify the core values that have guided you and think about how they align with potential award categories.
4. Use these exercises to construct a personal brand statement that succinctly communicates your unique offerings.

Engaging in self-assessment and gathering feedback from peers can provide additional insights into your strengths and areas for improvement. This will refine your personal narrative and prepare you for future opportunities. Remember, the process of building a strong personal brand is ongoing and evolves as you grow professionally.

It's helpful to create a portfolio that documents your work and achievements. This will make it easier to showcase your skills when applying for awards. Use social media and professional networks to amplify your brand, share your story, and engage with others in your field. This active presence reinforces your brand identity and increases your visibility among peers and industry leaders.

Pursuing awards is a strategic aspect of personal brand development. When approached thoughtfully, they offer more than just recognition—they validate your efforts, bolster your reputation, and open doors to new opportunities. Each recognition you receive is a testament to your trajectory and a stepping stone toward greater accomplishments.

By understanding and articulating what distinguishes you, embracing your core values, and confidently presenting your expertise, you lay the groundwork for a robust personal brand.

Awards then become a goal and a reflection of your sustained excellence and dedication. In this process, authenticity and consistency in representing your brand are key, allowing you to leave a lasting impact on those around you and strengthen your standing in your profession.

Aligning Brand Image with Award Criteria

Developing a personal brand through the strategic pursuit of awards can significantly enhance your professional profile. However, to be effective, you must tailor your branding efforts to the specific requirements of each award. Grasping the distinct expectations of each award ensures that your achievements and contributions are showcased in a manner that resonates with the judges while elevating your overall brand perception.

The initial step in connecting your brand with targeted awards involves thoroughly investigating the award criteria. Each award has unique prerequisites, encompassing particular achievements, experiences, or attributes sought in candidates. Dedicating time to comprehend these elements is essential, as it allows you to customize your application, highlighting aspects of your journey that fulfill or surpass the award's standards. For instance, if an award seeks to acknowledge innovation in digital marketing strategies, showcasing your groundbreaking project that transformed your company's online interactions can illustrate your compatibility with the award's mission. This careful customization of applications boosts your chances of winning and reinforces your personal brand as intentional and focused.

In addition to examining the criteria, synchronizing your brand messaging with the award's goals is vital. Every interaction—whether a written application or interview—should consistently convey both your brand's core values and mission, as well as the purpose of the award. This entails meticulously crafting your narratives and statements to ensure they resonate with the awarding organization's values while remaining authentic to your brand identity. In doing so, you foster a powerful connection between what the award symbolizes and your own principles, strengthening your standing within the context of the prize. For example, in pursuing an award prioritizing community leadership, your communications should highlight how your personal initiatives have positively impacted communities, reflecting shared ideals.

Showcasing relevant experiences in your award submissions is another crucial aspect. Present your past roles, projects, and accomplishments according to the award's criteria, clearly establishing your suitability as a candidate. This strategic depiction of experiences goes beyond enumerating achievements; it involves narrating how those experiences exemplify the attributes or skills the award aims to honor. If the award focuses on sustainability, explain how your leadership in an eco-friendly initiative led to measurable environmental benefits, clearly showing how your efforts match the award's objectives. Such narratives substantiate your application and enhance your brand by presenting you as a visionary and results-oriented individual.

Equally significant is maintaining a cohesive visual identity across all nomination materials. Visual consistency extends beyond aesthetics, incorporating the deliberate choice of colors, fonts, and images that embody your brand. The visual representation should match your established brand aesthetics, enhancing recognition and leaving a lasting impression on evaluators. This coherence across materials—from your resume to presentation slides—solidifies your brand identity and showcases professionalism and meticulousness, qualities highly valued in any competitive award environment. By synchronizing these visual elements with the award's themes or characteristics, such as utilizing eco-friendly imagery for an environmentally conscious award, you further emphasize your commitment to the cause and brand credibility.

Throughout this path, remember that cultivating a personal brand through awards is a continuous process requiring ongoing evaluation and improvement. As your career develops, consistently review and refine your personal brand identity to ensure it reflects evolving industry standards while embracing new opportunities and recognitions that arise. Regular assessments will help you remain true to your core values while adapting to future ambitions and achievements.

Leveraging Media Exposure Post-Award

Leveraging award recognition is a powerful strategy for amplifying your personal brand's visibility. After receiving an award, the next step is to efficaciously announce this achievement to ensure it resonates with your target audience. Social media platforms offer a dynamic avenue for sharing your success story. By crafting engaging posts highlighting the award's significance and what it means for your personal or professional career, you can create buzz and draw attention from relevant stakeholders like potential clients, employers, or collaborators. Craft your message to reflect the values and mission of the award, offering followers insight into how this recognition fits into your overarching brand narrative.

Once you've announced your achievement, integrating your award into marketing materials becomes important. Awards are trust signals that augment your credibility, making them invaluable components of your brand communications. For instance, updating your biography on networking sites or your personal website to include this recognition showcases your accomplishments and signifies a level of expertise and dedication to excellence. This strengthens existing relationships and can attract new opportunities as people recognize the value and quality associated with your brand. Ensure that the visual representation of the award aligns with your brand's aesthetics, whether in email signatures, brochures, or digital portfolios, maintaining consistency across all mediums.

Engaging with media outlets is another effective way to position yourself as a thought leader post-award. By pitching your story to industry publications or reaching out to journalists who focus on your field, you open doors to articles or interviews that can extend your reach beyond your immediate network. When communicating with the press, focus on the unique angle of your victory—was the award due to innovative projects, community impact, or outstanding leadership? Highlight these aspects to demonstrate why your story matters, reinforcing your standing as an authority and advancing your brand narrative through credible third-party endorsement.

Creating content around your award can further strengthen your connection with your audience, establishing you as a knowledgeable authority in your area of expertise. Consider producing blog posts, podcasts, or videos discussing the path toward achieving the award, the challenges faced, and the lessons learned along the way. This content serves multiple purposes: it provides valuable insights to those aspiring to similar achievements, offers a behind-the-scenes look at your work ethic and determination, and fosters a deeper relationship with your audience as they engage with authentic narratives. Interactive content, such as Q&A sessions or live discussions about your field triggered by the award, can also drive engagement and boost visibility.

Incorporate guidelines consistently to maximize the positive impact of your awards on your brand:

1. Announce your achievement on social media with a message that resonates with your audience's interests and reflects your brand's values and the award's purpose.
2. Showcase your award in all relevant marketing materials to bolster your credibility and attract new opportunities. Engage media outlets to broaden your reach and establish your reputation as a thought leader by presenting compelling angles of your award story to gain media traction.
3. Create diverse content formats, from detailed blogs to

interactive videos, to share the insights gained from your journey and connect deeply with your audience, solidifying your authority in your field.

Summary and Reflections

Pursuing awards is far more than a validation of accomplishments—it is a strategic avenue for building and amplifying your personal brand. Throughout this chapter, we've examined how the synergy between your unique strengths and values and the awards you pursue can create a compelling professional narrative. Awards serve as powerful credibility markers, offering tangible evidence of your expertise while shaping how you are perceived within your industry. They reflect your core values, reinforcing an authentic image that resonates with both colleagues and potential clients or partners.

You create a strategic approach that highlights your commitment and expertise by clearly defining what sets you apart and connecting these qualities with the right honors. This elevates your profile and demonstrates your relevance and leadership in your field. Awards become a mirror that reflects your experience—one built on resilience, growth, and dedication to excellence.

However, integrating awards into your brand strategy is a process that requires ongoing reflection and recalibration. As the industry landscape shifts, so too should your approach.

Regularly reassessing your brand against emerging trends and opportunities ensures you remain at the forefront, continuously signaling that you are prepared for the next big step. The trophies on your shelf are not just reminders of past achievements—they are stepping stones toward future leadership, greater responsibilities, and further recognition.

However, awards are only one part of the equation. What happens when the right connections come into play? How do networking and relationships fuel your trajectory to award-winning success? In the next chapter, we'll explore the vital role that networking plays in uncovering and seizing award opportunities—because sometimes, who you know is just as important as what you've done.

6

Networking to Enhance Award Opportunities

What if the key to winning an award wasn't just about your achievements but who you knew? In the competitive race for recognition, it's easy to think that success depends solely on your individual accomplishments. However, the truth is that relationships can often be the deciding factor that tips the scales in your favor. Imagine having someone in your corner who knows the ropes—someone who has been a winner, a juror, or an insider in the industry. Wouldn't their guidance and connections give you a significant edge?

This chapter invites you to look beyond your application and explore the untapped potential of your network. Building strategic relationships isn't just an optional bonus—it can be the secret ingredient that elevates your entry from incredible to unforgettable. Ready to discover how powerful connections can change the trajectory of your award path? Let's dive in.

Connecting with Past Winners and Jurors

Networking to enhance award opportunities involves more than just connecting with people; it's about forming strategic alliances that can provide critical insights and support to improve your award application success rates. One of the most effective ways to do this is by learning from past winners and jurors, who offer invaluable perspectives on what it takes to stand out in a competitive landscape.

Firstly, engaging with past winners provides unique insights into strategies that have proven successful. These individuals have navigated the complex process of award applications and emerged victorious, making their experiences incredibly valuable. Perhaps they tailored their applications to highlight specific accomplishments or framed their narratives to resonate with the judging panel. Learning these strategies can help refine your approach, giving you an edge over other applicants. Past winners are often candid about common pitfalls and obstacles they faced. By understanding these challenges, you can anticipate potential issues and develop strategies to avoid them, ensuring a smoother application process.

A practical guideline here would be to seek opportunities to engage with past winners through interviews, workshops, or networking events where these individuals share their experiences. Listening to their stories can provide firsthand knowledge that textbooks or online guides cannot match. Consider even reaching out directly via professional networks like LinkedIn to ask specific questions about their journeys.

Engaging with award jurors offers a direct line to understanding the judging criteria and gaining application feedback. Jurors have the unique vantage point of having reviewed countless applications, making them experts in distinguishing between a good application and a great one. Building relationships with these professionals lets you gather insights into what makes an application stand out. Whether it's the clarity of presentation, the impact of achievements, or the cohesiveness of the personal narrative, jurors can guide you in fine-tuning your submission.

It's helpful to attend panels, talks, or webinars where jurors discuss their judging processes and criteria openly. These interactions can demystify the selection process, clarify how decisions are made, and help you align your application to better meet expectations. Incorporating feedback mechanisms after engaging with jurors can refine your approach further. For instance, some events offer critique sessions or Q&A opportunities where you can present aspects of your application for direct feedback. Use these opportunities to iterate and improve your submissions continuously.

Building connections also opens doors to alliances, leading to mentorship and support opportunities. Developing strong ties with industry leaders, peers, and past recipients can create a robust support system. Mentorship stands out as a significant asset of these alliances. An experienced mentor can offer personalized advice, helping you maneuver the complexities of your career path and award applications. They can guide everything from crafting compelling narratives to efficiently communicating your achievements.

Here's a guideline:

1. Actively seek mentors within your network with a track record of similar successes.
2. Establish regular communication channels to encourage these relationships, whether through formal mentoring programs or informal coffee chats.
3. Mentorship is not a one-way street; mutual respect and value exchange reinforce long-lasting alliances.

Finally, creating a community with past recipients encourages sharing resources and motivation, encouraging an environment of collective growth. Such communities can serve as platforms to exchange information on best practices, celebrate wins, and maintain momentum throughout the award experience. Building connections in these circles can reveal hidden opportunities, such as collaborative projects, joint applications, or referrals, which might not be accessible otherwise.

To cultivate this community, participate in forums, discussion groups, or online communities focused on awards and recognitions in your field. These spaces are ideal for exchanging experiences, getting peer reviews, and finding cheerleaders who encourage you every step of the way. Sharing your lessons with newcomers can also solidify your place in these communities, as generosity typically breeds reciprocation.

Utilizing Social Media to Share Successes

In today's digital age, social media has become indispensable for building and showcasing a professional brand. This section emphasizes the importance of using these platforms strategically to highlight one's achievements, enhancing visibility and credibility in the industry. For professionals looking to increase their chances of winning awards, crafting a robust presence on platforms like LinkedIn elevates professional visibility and attracts attention from key stakeholders in your field.

A well-constructed social media profile is a virtual resume projecting authority and expertise. By showcasing skills, accomplishments, and milestones, individuals can draw in opportunities and form valuable connections. When it comes to awards, it's important to ensure your profile is updated with relevant wins and recognitions. This not only bolsters your image but also signals your ongoing commitment to excellence. A clear guideline for crafting such a presence involves regularly updating profiles, seeking endorsements, and sharing insightful content that supports your career goals.

Beyond personal branding, a productive engagement strategy on social media is pivotal in linking you with industry leaders and potential jurors who might be instrumental in award decisions. Engaging actively means posting updates, participating in discussions, commenting thoughtfully on others' posts, and sharing industry news or articles relevant to your field. These actions establish you as a thought leader and keep you in the loop with current trends and conversations. For instance, joining groups related to your industry can provide insights into upcoming awards and events while interacting with leading figures, which opens doors to mentorship and endorsement. It's about creating a dialogue rather than a monologue, where genuine interactions pave the way for collaborative opportunities.

Highlighting your wins on these platforms significantly fosters community support and strengthens connections within your network. Sharing achievements shouldn't come across as boasting; instead, it should be seen as an opportunity to inspire and engage your audience. For young professionals and business owners alike, reflecting on what these successes mean personally and professionally can resonate well with peers and superiors alike. Furthermore, acknowledging collaborators who contributed to your success is a great way to solidify relationships. Such gratitude often results in reciprocated support when you need it most, particularly during award applications or nominations.

Creating content around your award experience is another strategic move that can pay dividends in terms of visibility and professional growth. Content creation could range from blog posts and videos discussing what the award entails, why it's important, and how you've prepared to podcasts or webinars sharing lessons learned during the process. This educates your audience and attracts potential collaborators who see value in being associated with your dedication and drive. Sharing behind-the-scenes experiences and challenges encountered along the way humanizes your path, making it relatable and inspiring to others in your industry.

As you craft this content, consider the audience it reaches and tailor it to meet their interests and needs. Simple storytelling techniques, including overcoming obstacles, persistent effort, and eventual success, resonate well. The goal is to broadcast achievements and build a narrative that positions you as both an achiever and a learner. It's about convincing your audience—even those outside your immediate network—that your journey holds insights applicable to their own paths, thereby enlarging your professional sphere of influence.

Attending Industry Events for Exposure

Attending events is a foundational strategy for effective relationship-building, mainly when aiming to improve your visibility and opportunities within your professional community. Imagine walking into a room buzzing with ambition and potential; every handshake could be the beginning of a new venture or collaboration. The vibrancy of networking events lies in their ability to bring together diverse minds from various fields, each eager to connect and share insights. Such gatherings are indispensable for meeting influential figures and establishing yourself as a noteworthy player in your sector.

Building connections at these events provides an invaluable opportunity to interact directly with key influencers who can open doors to collaborations you might not have imagined possible. For instance, engaging in genuine conversations with leaders in your industry can lead to partnerships or projects that align with your goals. Imagine attending a tech conference where you discuss emerging trends over coffee with a renowned digital innovator whose next project could benefit from your expertise. These serendipitous encounters are the essence of productive networking.

These events allow you to build and augment your visibility. Sharing your achievements and insights publicly at such forums does wonders in positioning yourself as a trusted authority in your area of expertise. When you step onto a panel discussion or lead a workshop, you're putting your skills and knowledge on display, boosting your credibility and making you a magnet for future opportunities. For example, imagine speaking at a business seminar and being approached afterward by attendees who resonate with your perspective and want to collaborate or seek advice.

Events are not just about making connections but also about learning and growing. Workshops and seminars often accompany these gatherings, offering deep dives into current trends and strategies relevant to your field. Participating in these activities refines your understanding and keeps you updated with the latest industry shifts. It's like attending a master class where you not only absorb knowledge but also get to ask questions and gain practical insights that you can apply immediately, perhaps transforming how you approach upcoming award applications or business strategies.

The true magic of attending these events unfolds post-event, during follow-up engagements. Meeting someone is just the start; maintaining these connections is where relationships flourish. A conversation shared over lunch can become a long-term mentorship if nurtured correctly. Following up with personalized emails or LinkedIn messages can help you maintain the momentum from the initial meeting. Expressing appreciation for the interaction and proposing future touchpoints to keep the dialogue going is important. This consistent engagement indicates professionalism and proactivity, which leave a lasting impression.

Consider the scenario where you send a thoughtful message to a business leader you met after attending a major conference, referencing a topic you both found intriguing. In doing so, you remind them of the connection you made and showcase your interest in their insights, paving the path for a collaborative relationship or even future mentorship. This practice of following up transforms fleeting event interactions into robust networks that can support your career advancement over time.

To maximize the benefits of relationship-building events, it's wise to approach them with a strategy. Begin by setting clear objectives for what you hope to achieve at each event, whether connecting with specific individuals, gaining insight into particular topics, or elevating your brand recognition. Having clear goals enables you to focus your energy competently.

Once at the event, make a conscious effort to engage authentically. Listen actively to others, pose insightful questions, and exchange ideas openly. This authenticity enables trust and respect, forming the foundation of strong professional relationships. Remember, building connections is not about taking but sharing. As you navigate through different discussions, offer your expertise and help to those who might need it, laying the groundwork for reciprocal support.

Insights and Implications

This chapter highlights the powerful role of strategic relationship-building in enhancing award success by fostering connections that provide valuable insights and guidance. Building alliances with past winners and learning directly from jurors offer unique perspectives on crafting standout submissions while engaging in mentorships supports personal and professional development. Additionally, leveraging social media and attending industry events are essential for increasing visibility; they enable you to create an engaging online presence and spark face-to-face connections that can lead to lasting partnerships. Building these relationships is far more than gathering contacts—it's about cultivating a community that supports and amplifies your success, helping to turn aspirations into tangible achievements and opening doors to future opportunities.

But what happens when inevitable setbacks occur? How do you maintain momentum when facing rejection or disappointment on this journey? As you prepare to leverage your network to its fullest, emotional resilience becomes critical in navigating the ups and downs of pursuing awards. In the next chapter, we'll explore emotional resilience's vital role in sustaining your professional growth. Setbacks are not just part of the process but stepping stones to your ultimate success.

7

Emotional Resilience and Professional Growth

Imagine standing at a crossroads in your career, faced with a setback just as you aim to secure recognition for your work. In moments like these, emotional resilience becomes essential. Building resilience isn't just about enduring challenges; it's about learning to harness these experiences to fuel your path toward success and visibility. For those seeking awards and recognition as a catalyst for career or business growth, resilience provides the foundation to persevere through setbacks, rejections, and unforeseen obstacles that arise along the path to acclaim.

Emotional resilience enables you to reframe setbacks as valuable learning opportunities, helping you stay motivated despite fierce competition. Adopting a growth-focused mindset makes you more adaptable and resourceful—qualities necessary for navigating the demanding process of pursuing awards. Building supportive networks and employing strategies to cope with rejection while maintaining motivation during adversity can help you achieve a balanced outlook. This balance allows you to remain engaged and persistent. As you develop these strategies, you'll discover that resilience is one of your most valuable assets, guiding you through the highs and lows of striving for recognition that elevates careers and businesses.

Developing Coping Strategies for Rejection

Rejection is a shared human experience that we all encounter at various points in our personal and professional lives. Yet, it's not the experience of rejection that defines us but how we respond to it. By exploring practical strategies for navigating rejection, we can transform this challenging experience into an opportunity for growth and resilience.

A key element in handling rejection efficiently is embracing a growth mindset. This approach involves viewing setbacks not as failures but as valuable learning opportunities. For instance, when a job application is denied, or a project proposal is turned down, consider what lessons can be extracted from the experience instead of dwelling on the disappointment. It might be a chance to reassess your approach, improve your skills, or gain a deeper understanding of your field. Psychologist Carol Dweck's work on growth mindsets emphasizes the importance of seeing challenges as stepping stones to improvement rather than obstacles. Reframing negative experiences as part of a broader learning experience can foster resilience and maintain motivation.

Practicing self-compassion is another vital strategy in dealing with rejection. Our instinctive reaction to rejection often is self-criticism, which can erode self-esteem and reinforce negative feelings. Instead, self-kindness can help mitigate these effects, encouraging a more positive internal dialogue. Treat yourself with the same empathy and understanding that you would offer a friend in similar circumstances. This practice helps preserve self-esteem and shifts your focus towards recognizing personal strengths, even amidst setbacks. Research by Dr. Kristin Neff suggests that self-compassion plays an essential role in buffering against the negative impacts of rejection, helping individuals maintain a sense of self-worth despite external evaluations (Saxena, 2023).

Journaling reflections can be a powerful tool for processing emotions related to rejection. This practice allows individuals to explore their feelings in a structured way, facilitating emotional clarity and stress management. Through regular journaling, you can analyze emotions, identify patterns in your reactions, and develop constructive responses to rejection. Writing about experiences can provide insights that are not immediately apparent, enabling you to view situations from different perspectives and devise new strategies for moving forward. In addition, this reflective practice can enhance emotional resilience by offering a safe space to vent frustrations and brainstorm potential improvements.

Seeking support networks is equally important in managing feelings of rejection. Sharing experiences with friends, family, or colleagues can provide validation and fresh perspectives. Discussing your feelings with others who have faced similar situations can help normalize the experience of rejection and reduce feelings of isolation. Support networks also enable community resilience, creating an environment where challenges are understood as common hurdles rather than personal failures. Engaging with a supportive community can offer guidance, encouragement, and new ideas for navigating difficult times. If necessary, professional support from therapists or counselors can also be invaluable in addressing deep-seated emotional responses to rejection (7 Ways to Effectively Reframe Rejection, 2023).

Among these strategies, cultivating a growth mindset stands out for its foundational impact on emotional resilience. When we perceive rejection as one path among many, we empower ourselves to explore alternative routes and adapt to new circumstances. This mental flexibility forms the core of resilience, equipping us with the perseverance to pursue long-term goals despite setbacks. Ultimately, recognizing rejection as an intrinsic part of the professional career can lessen its sting, allowing us to forge ahead with renewed determination.

Reflecting on each of these strategies reveals their interconnected nature: self-compassion fosters a growth mindset; journaling aids in self-reflection; support networks reinforce both personal resilience and collective strength. Together, they create a comprehensive framework for transforming rejection into an impetus for growth. By integrating these practices into daily life, individuals can constructively navigate rejection, maintaining momentum in their pursuit of personal and professional development.

Maintaining Motivation Through Adversity

Pursuing awards is rarely a straight path—there will be obstacles, setbacks, and moments of doubt. Yet, the ability to maintain motivation through these challenges often sets award-winning professionals and businesses apart. Intrinsic motivation—the internal drive to pursue goals because of personal meaning and satisfaction—is important in sustaining momentum, even when the odds seem stacked against you. In the context of applying for awards, this motivation fuels the persistence needed to refine submissions, seek feedback, and continue striving for excellence after each setback.

Setting milestones is one of the most productive ways to maintain motivation throughout this process. Just as applying for prestigious industry awards requires a long-term commitment, breaking down this journey into smaller, manageable steps helps keep you focused and engaged. For example, instead of solely focusing on winning the award, you can celebrate milestones like completing the research phase, submitting a polished draft, or securing a mentor's feedback. Each milestone achieved provides an opportunity for reflection and celebration, reaffirming your progress and keeping you motivated for the next step in the process.

Positive affirmation practices can further sustain your motivation when pursuing recognition. As you refine your award submissions or seek out new growth opportunities, affirmations like "My work is worthy of recognition" or "I am capable of achieving this goal" can reinforce your confidence, particularly during moments of self-doubt. Awards applications can sometimes feel daunting, but positive self-talk can reshape your mindset, ensuring you stay motivated and resilient despite the inevitable challenges.

Similarly, visualizing success can help maintain motivation, especially when the awards process becomes demanding or competitive. By vividly imagining yourself winning an award, giving an acceptance speech, or seeing your business featured as a leader in the industry, you strengthen your commitment to turning these aspirations into reality. Visualization connects your intrinsic motivation to the tangible outcome of receiving awards, making the hard work leading up to that moment more rewarding.

Finally, creating accountability structures can help ensure you stay on track as you pursue recognition. Whether through regular check-ins with mentors, peer support groups, or even setting personal deadlines for different stages of your awards application, accountability keeps you committed to the process. Knowing that others are invested in your success can help keep your motivation high, driving you to overcome the challenges that arise along the way.

When these strategies—setting milestones, practicing affirmations, visualizing success, and establishing accountability—are combined, they form a comprehensive system that helps you remain resilient, motivated, and focused on the path to winning awards. Ultimately, this sustained motivation transforms adversity into an opportunity for growth, leading to personal transformation and the recognition that can propel your career or business forward.

Incorporating Stress-Reduction Techniques

The journey toward winning professional awards and recognition can be rewarding and demanding. The high standards and intense competition often bring stress that, if not managed, can hinder your performance and overall progress. Incorporating stress-reduction techniques into your daily routine is necessary for maintaining mental health. Still, it can also improve your ability to perform at your best in your field—whether preparing an award submission, leading a significant project, or pursuing career growth.

One powerful way to reduce stress and build emotional resilience throughout this process is through the practice of mindfulness. Mindfulness encourages professionals to remain present and grounded, preventing them from becoming overwhelmed by deadlines, expectations, or competition pressures. For example, if you're preparing an application for a prestigious industry award, practicing mindfulness meditation can help clear your mind, allowing for sharper focus and better decision-making. By focusing on the present moment rather than worrying about potential outcomes, you position yourself to handle challenges more effectively, increasing the likelihood of producing high-quality work that stands out.

In addition to mindfulness, physical activity serves as a critical stress management tool. Regular exercise boosts endorphin levels, leading to improved mood and greater mental clarity—key elements when preparing for or competing in award submissions. For instance, taking a break from work to engage in a brief exercise routine, such as walking or stretching, can refresh your mind and enhance your creativity. This physical well-being translates into professional growth, as a well-balanced and healthy individual is better equipped to tackle the long hours and intense focus required to pursue recognition.

Establishing healthy boundaries is also vital during the award application process. When striving for recognition, it's easy to overcommit or push yourself beyond your limits. Setting clear boundaries helps ensure that you maintain balance, protect your energy, and prevent burnout. Whether you are leading a team through a major project or submitting individual work for a professional accolade, defining when to step back and recharge is crucial for sustaining high performance. For example, learning to say no to additional tasks or setting aside non-negotiable time for rest can help you approach your work with greater focus and determination, ultimately increasing your chances of success.

Engaging in hobbies offers another way to manage stress and rejuvenate your creative energy. Pursuing personal interests outside your professional work can provide a mental reset, making it easier to return to your award goals with renewed vigor. Hobbies like painting, playing music, or gardening offer relaxation and a creative outlet, which can inspire fresh ideas for award submissions or presentations. Many successful professionals find that their most innovative solutions come to them during these leisure moments, making hobbies a crucial part of stress reduction and creative growth.

Integrating these stress-reduction techniques into your daily routine improves your well-being and positions yourself for greater success. Managing stress allows you to remain resilient and focused on your path to recognition, enabling you to deliver your best work and increase your chances of earning prestigious awards that can accelerate your professional and business growth.

Concluding Thoughts

In this chapter, we've looked into the power of emotional resilience in managing rejection and setbacks. From adopting a growth mindset to embracing self-compassion, each strategy helps you turn challenges into stepping stones toward personal and professional growth. Rejections aren't roadblocks but opportunities to learn, adapt, and improve. Whether through journaling to process emotions or leaning on support networks for shared wisdom, you're better equipped to remain focused and motivated on your path to success.

Building emotional resilience isn't just about overcoming obstacles—it's also about maintaining the momentum needed to keep striving for recognition. Bouncing back from setbacks is important in achieving your long-term professional goals, primarily as you pursue prestigious industry awards that can elevate your career or business. Every rejection can be reframed as valuable feedback, refining your approach and sharpening your strategy for future recognition.

But resilience alone is not enough. In the upcoming chapter, we'll uncover how receiving recognition can reshape your professional identity, open doors to new possibilities, and set the stage for even greater achievements.

What happens when the world acknowledges your efforts? Join me in the next chapter as we explore the Transformative Power of Recognition—and discover how it can propel your trajectory to new heights.

8

Transformative Power of Recognition

Imagine this: you've just received a prestigious award in your field, and suddenly, doors that seemed shut for years are opening wide. Your network is expanding, opportunities are multiplying, and your credibility has skyrocketed. This isn't just a fleeting moment of applause— it's the beginning of a lasting transformation. The power of recognition goes beyond trophies and accolades; it has the potential to reshape your career trajectory and redefine your organization's place in the market. Awards create a ripple effect, igniting confidence, building trust, and propelling you toward new realms of achievement. The question is: how can you harness this power and make it work for you?

More than a feel-good moment, recognition can catalyze growth, impacting both the individual and the broader organization. The ripple effect of recognition can fuel deeper motivation, driving people to push beyond their previous limits. In a world where visibility and credibility are highly prized, receiving an award can offer that golden spotlight, shining on the hard work and dedication that often goes unseen. But beyond this initial gleam lies a more profound transformation, one that reshapes mindsets and infuses fresh vigor into professional pursuits. Young professionals aiming to establish their personal brands find great value in these recognitions as they enter the competitive stage. Similarly, seasoned business owners regard awards as opportunities to refresh their brand's identity and assert their standing within the industry. Feelings of validation and acknowledgment usher in a refreshing wave of motivation, pushing recipients to raise the bar for themselves and others around them.

Join me in exploring how powerful storytelling around achievements can inspire peers and why aligning awards with core values strengthens organizational identity and mission. Whether you're looking to make a mark in your career or elevate your business's reputation, this exploration of the transformative power of recognition offers valuable insights and practical strategies.

Increasing Motivation Through Achievement

Recognition from awards is a vital element in enhancing intrinsic motivation and driving performance for both individuals and organizations. The act of acknowledging achievement doesn't merely serve as an external honor; it fundamentally validates the hard work and dedication that individuals pour into their endeavors, offering a powerful boost to their internal motivation. This recognition can create a cascading impact, fostering a culture of excellence where people feel valued and inspired to continue striving toward greater accomplishments. For young professionals and established business owners, acknowledging their efforts through awards can be transformational, providing both motivation and tangible evidence of their contributions.

Recognizing hard work serves as a pivotal tool for validating effort and boosting motivation. When individuals and teams receive recognition, it affirms that their hard work has not gone unnoticed. This validation encourages pride and fulfillment, reinforcing their commitment to their tasks. Such positivity enhances the willingness to engage with new challenges, confirming their skills and contributions are appreciated in their professional circles. Often, this validation comes in symbolic or formal awards, but it can be just as effective through simpler means, such as public acknowledgments or thank-you notes. O'Flaherty et al. (2021) highlight that even small gestures of recognition can significantly improve employee motivation and morale when tailored to fit unique organizational contexts.

Pursuing awards encourages individuals and teams to surpass their previous limits, pushing them to achieve more than they initially thought possible. Awards present a clear goal that requires focused effort and innovation to attain. In aiming for such recognition, individuals stretch beyond their regular duties, exploring creative solutions and refining their skills to reach new performance heights. This journey toward achieving an award catalyzes growth, pushing boundaries, and instilling a continuous improvement mindset in a team. For instance, consider a tech startup aiming for industry recognition through an innovation award. The mere prospect of gaining this external validation can drive team members to collaborate more competently, improve productivity, and support original ideas, all aimed at setting themselves apart from competitors.

Celebrating achievements through awards is closely linked with improved employee morale and engagement. When successes are acknowledged with awards, it brings about a collective celebration that boosts the entire team's spirit. These celebrations reinforce positive behavior and promote a strong sense of belonging and camaraderie among team members. The emotional uplift associated with awards can invigorate workplace dynamics, leading to higher levels of engagement and satisfaction. Ensuring regular award ceremonies or recognition moments in an organization can help maintain high morale, encouraging employees to remain committed and passionate about their roles. Creating such recognition-rich environments requires thoughtful implementation, aligning with the idea that attention to detail and the presence of symbolic awards can significantly amplify motivation, as noted by Bi Worldwide (2023).

Sharing success stories is instrumental in inspiring colleagues to pursue goals ambitiously. When individuals who have achieved award-winning projects share their journeys and experiences, it delivers a powerful message to peers. These narratives showcase the possibilities that arise from hard work and dedication, igniting a spark in others to reach similar heights. By highlighting overcoming obstacles and celebrating victories, these stories encourage a mindset where perseverance and ambition become contagious. In a workplace setting, storytelling around awards can be incorporated into meetings or newsletters, creating an environment where sharing and learning from others' successes is embedded in the culture. Showcasing diverse pathways to success inspires and provides concrete examples that others can emulate in their pursuit of personal and professional goals.

Shaping Company Culture with Recognition

In the sphere of organizational development, awards significantly contribute to cultivating a positive, high-performing culture. Let us examine how consistent recognition fosters an environment where every individual contribution is appreciated and acknowledged.

Consistent recognition fosters a culture of appreciation throughout all levels of an organization. It diminishes hierarchical barriers, encouraging feelings of equality and belonging among employees. When efforts are regularly acknowledged, employees are inspired to give their best and assured that their contributions matter. This practice promotes open dialogue and motivates teams to collaborate towards shared objectives. Organizations prioritizing consistent recognition experience heightened employee engagement, increasing productivity and job satisfaction. Such companies benefit from lower turnover rates as employees derive satisfaction from their roles, establishing a stable and nurturing workplace atmosphere.

Awards given to teams highlight the significance of collective success, fostering camaraderie and solidarity among members. Honoring teams for meeting or surpassing goals emphasizes the value of collaboration and shared objectives. Team awards create shared moments of triumph, allowing individuals to recognize one another's strengths and support each other's development. This cultural reinforcement fortifies team relationships and connects personal aspirations with broader organizational ambitions. By establishing common goals and celebrating successes collectively, an organization nurtures a spirit of unity and collaboration—key qualities for achieving enduring success.

Linking awards with core values serves as an effective tool for reinforcing an organization's mission and vision. When recognition programs reflect the company's foundational principles, employees forge a stronger connection with their work. Core values evolve beyond mere words, transforming into guiding principles that inform behavior and decision-making in the organization. For instance, if innovation is a core principle, rewarding creative solutions and novel ideas can prompt employees to approach challenges inventively. Associating awards with these values highlights accomplishments and reinforces the organization's commitment to its principles, thereby cultivating trust and loyalty among its workforce.

Diversity and inclusion are essential aspects of contemporary workplace culture, and acknowledging diverse talents is crucial for fostering an inclusive environment. Award systems that celebrate the unique contributions of individuals from various backgrounds convey a vital message: diversity is embraced and utilized to spur innovation. By valuing different perspectives and experiences, organizations can tap into a broader range of ideas and strategies, resulting in more inventive solutions and adaptable practices. Awards that recognize these various contributions serve as catalysts for creative thinking and motivate employees to leverage their rich backgrounds in contributing to the company's success.

To effectively nurture a culture of recognition, organizations require structured approaches. Establish formal recognition programs that specify criteria and processes for distributing awards. Promote transparency and fairness by including various voices in the decision-making process. Strengthen team cohesion through collective celebrations and activities that highlight shared goals. Integrate workshops or training sessions to assist employees in connecting personal objectives with team and organizational missions. Encourage open discussions about the core values that support recognition, making them accessible and meaningful to all staff. Promote inclusivity by inviting nominations from various employees to ensure varied representation. Regular assessments and feedback mechanisms can enhance these programs, ensuring they remain effective and fair.

Paving the Way for Future Opportunities

Awards have long been significant across various sectors, acting as a beacon that draws attention to the accomplishments of individuals and organizations. For young professionals eager to carve out their niche or established businesses looking to refresh their reputations, awards present an invaluable opportunity for growth and transformation. Winning an award increases visibility, making it a pivotal moment in the career trajectory of many, but beyond the trophy or accolade, the true value lies in the doors they open.

When someone wins a highly recognized award, it instantly raises their profile in the industry. This heightened visibility is important for creating opportunities that otherwise might remain inaccessible. For instance, industry leaders often take note of award winners, setting the stage for introductions to key players and facilitating valuable and enriching networking connections. These connections can be transformative, offering insights, mentorship, and partnerships that drive personal and professional growth.

Recognition through awards can naturally lead to new partnerships and collaborations. When an individual or organization earns an honor, it validates their expertise and achievements, enhancing their credibility in the eyes of others. Partners and collaborators prefer to work with those who have proven themselves capable; awards serve as this validation. In a world where trust and credibility are paramount, an award can act as a seal of approval, reassuring potential partners of one's capabilities. This can pave the way for collaborative projects that align with strategic goals, helping to amplify success through shared efforts.

Regarding career advancement, awards function as credible markers that influence future trajectories. They provide tangible proof of one's skills and accomplishments, which can be particularly persuasive when negotiating promotions or seeking new roles. Employers are more likely to offer advanced positions to candidates with a track record of recognized excellence. For young professionals, boasting such achievements on a résumé can differentiate them from competitors, giving them an edge in a crowded job market.

Similarly, awards strengthen personal and company branding significantly. Winning an award places individuals and companies in the spotlight, showcasing their strengths where potential clients and stakeholders may be watching. Strong branding resonates with audiences, instilling a sense of trust and reliability. As a result, companies that capitalize on award recognition can attract clients drawn by the promise of quality service or product that the award signifies. Personal branding follows a similar trajectory; professionals recognized with awards can leverage this to position themselves as thought leaders, attracting speaking engagements or consulting offers.

The ripple effect of winning awards extends into longer-term impacts by nurturing inspiration and aspiration among peers. When one person receives recognition, it sets a standard and encourages others to strive for similar success. Organizations that highlight employee achievements facilitate a culture that rewards excellence, motivating others to pursue excellence and contribute meaningfully to the business's mission.

However, navigating the award landscape involves strategic consideration. It's not merely about recognition but understanding how to maximize the benefits post-award. Leveraging media platforms is one aspect where guideline implementation becomes essential. Sharing news of the win through press releases, social media, and other communication channels further amplifies visibility, engages broader audiences, and underscores the achievement. This publicity can generate buzz, inviting inquiries from journalists interested in covering stories of success, thus expanding reach.

Moreover, becoming a role model—another area necessitating careful guidelines—requires maintaining integrity and continuing to deliver on the promises the award signifies. Resting on laurels is insufficient; a continuous effort to uphold high standards guarantees that the recognition remains relevant and deserved. The behavior and results expected of an award winner help raise expectations and set benchmarks for others to emulate, thereby influencing organizational norms positively.

Final Insights

This chapter explores the transformative power of awards and recognition as catalysts for personal and organizational growth. Awards boost motivation, promote a culture of excellence, and create pathways to future opportunities. Acknowledgment drives individuals and teams to exceed their limits and strengthens morale, fostering a sense of belonging and engagement within an organization. For young professionals and established business owners, strategically leveraging awards can enhance career trajectories and brand reputation, opening doors to collaborations and advancements.

Awards also shape company culture by aligning individual motivations with organizational goals, fostering an inclusive, celebratory environment. Embracing the potential of awards and recognition allows individuals and organizations to build lasting credibility and influence, ensuring sustained growth and success.

But how do you make the most of that recognition? Winning an award is just the beginning. The next chapter will explore leveraging these accolades to drive business growth and open doors to new possibilities. From marketing strategies to expanding your network, we'll uncover the steps you need to take to ensure your award wins are celebrated and translated into tangible results. Are you ready to turn recognition into real-world success? Let's dive in.

9

Leveraging Award Wins for Business Growth

Picture this: a single moment that can redefine your business trajectory, where the glimmer of a trophy not only celebrates your past accomplishments but also ignites a future brimming with possibilities. Winning an award can feel like stepping onto a larger stage, where the spotlight highlights your achievements and casts your business in a favorable light. The very first moment you clutch that trophy, it becomes more than just a symbol of success; it transforms into a powerful tool capable of opening doors, sparking conversations, and reimagining the future growth of your business. Leveraging these accolades effectively requires more than simply acknowledging them internally or displaying them proudly on your office shelf. It's about understanding how to integrate them seamlessly into your brand's narrative and marketing strategies so they resonate with clients, customers, and stakeholders alike. Awards have an intrinsic value—offering credibility and visibility—that can be harnessed through thoughtful planning and execution.

Whether you're a young professional looking to build a personal brand or an established business owner seeking innovative strategies, the following sections offer valuable insights designed to elevate your brand's standing and drive growth through award recognition.

Integrating Awards into Marketing Strategies

Leveraging award wins in your marketing campaigns can be a game-changer for emerging entrepreneurs and established businesses. Awards validate your hard work and significantly boost credibility and visibility. By strategically incorporating these honors into your marketing efforts, you can differentiate your brand and capture the attention of potential clients and investors.

Begin by prominently displaying award logos across all marketing materials. These symbols act as instant visual cues to potential customers, signaling quality and excellence. When people see an award logo on your brochures, flyers, or email signatures, it immediately sets your brand apart. It communicates that your business has been recognized for its outstanding innovation, service, and product quality contributions. Including such logos on print and digital marketing materials enhances your reputation and gives you a competitive edge in saturated markets. This small yet impactful addition can significantly influence customer perceptions and purchasing decisions.

Incorporating award achievements into advertising is also

important. Awards serve as endorsements from credible organizations, significantly increasing your brand's trustworthiness. For instance, a company featuring its latest award win in a TV commercial or digital ad campaign reinforces its market position and attracts new interest. It reassures existing customers while drawing in those who might be searching for reputable brands. The mention of awards in advertisements should be done creatively to maintain engagement rather than simply listing them. Consider using compelling narratives or testimonials highlighting how winning the award reflects your commitment to customer satisfaction and continuous improvement.

Regular website and social media platform updates are essential to inform your audience about your recent accolades. Websites are a hub for all brand-related information, so ensure your awards are highlighted on your homepage, About Us section, and other relevant pages. This visibility reinforces your brand's achievements every time someone visits. Similarly, sharing award news on social media helps increase your reach and engagement with audiences. Visual content showcasing the moment of your award acceptance and a post thanking customers for their support can create a positive buzz and foster a sense of community around your brand. Maintaining updated information on these platforms keeps your brand relevant and trustworthy in the eyes of digital-savvy consumers.

Using award wins as focal points in content marketing strategies can boost your marketing campaigns. Content marketing lets you narrate the story behind your brand's success, providing educational value while showcasing your expertise. Blog posts, videos, or podcasts discussing what the award signifies, overcoming challenges, and implementing innovations create deeper connections with your audience. You can even develop case studies or white papers on how your award-winning methods have benefited your clients. This approach positions you as an authoritative figure in your industry, which can be especially appealing to young professionals looking to learn from leading brands and established business owners seeking tried-and-tested practices.

To integrate these strategies effectively, consider developing guidelines that support consistency and cohesion across all channels. When highlighting award logos, choose placements that maximize visibility without overwhelming the overall design of your marketing materials. Design templates help maintain uniformity. In advertising, clearly articulate the story behind the award and connect it to your brand values to increase emotional engagement. Regularly update your website and social media profiles with fresh content related to awards by appointing a dedicated team member or using scheduling tools to streamline dissemination. Create an editorial calendar for content marketing that aligns award discussions with your broader marketing goals and client interests.

Expanding Reach through Public Relations

Leveraging award wins for your business isn't just about displaying trophies on a shelf. It's about turning those honors into powerful PR opportunities that elevate your brand's presence and influence. This section will guide you through effectively using these wins to generate robust public relations outcomes.

Crafting Press Releases: Once you've secured an award, the next step is communicating that success to a broader audience. A well-crafted press release serves as a bridge between your achievement and public recognition. To capture media interest, make your press release engaging and newsworthy by including compelling headlines and quotes from influential figures in your organization. Consistency in branding throughout the release helps reinforce your company's identity. When drafting the release, please focus on the details of the award and what it signifies for your company's progress and future goals. Including statistics or narratives illustrating the path to this recognition can provide journalists with the material they need for an engaging story, increasing the chances of coverage. You can also amplify the reach by sending it to industry-specific channels or utilizing online distribution services like PR Newswire to ensure it lands in the inboxes of key media players.

Engaging Influencers and Media: Award wins can be a unique opportunity to connect with influencers and media figures within your industry. Building relationships with these individuals can open doors to further recognition and promotional avenues. Reach out to influencers who align with your brand values or have a following that matches your target audience, sharing your achievement and how it reflects your company's ethos. Collaborations or partnerships can be formed where these influencers act as advocates for your brand, discussing your successes on their platforms. Similarly, leverage media contacts to create stories around your achievements. Engage with them through personalized pitches, emphasizing how the award positions your company as a leader in innovation or service excellence. Attending industry events where these media figures are present can also facilitate direct connections. By showing genuine interest in their work and communicating the impact of your award-winning efforts, you solidify your reputation as a credible and leading entity in your field.

Utilizing Online Newsrooms: Creating an online newsroom dedicated to showcasing your company's awards can significantly aid journalist outreach and public engagement. An accessible digital hub where media personnel can easily find information about your achievements streamlines the process of discovering your brand's strengths. Ensure the newsroom is regularly updated with detailed descriptions of each award, accompanying visuals, and links to relevant press releases. By categorizing content according to themes or timelines, you offer journalists ready-to-use resources that can be incorporated into broader narratives about your business or industry trends. Additionally, featuring testimonials or case studies related to the awards can provide deeper insights into your operations and values, adding layers to your public persona. Link this newsroom directly from your website's main navigation to maximize visibility and ease of access.

Hosting Award Celebration Events: Celebrating award wins through events is another strategic avenue to augment public relations. Such gatherings allow you to thank stakeholders and create buzz around your achievements. Consider hosting an event inviting clients, partners, media, and influencers to share your success. Whether it's a formal gala or an informal networking event, use the opportunity to highlight the award's significance and what it means for your future ambitions. Conduct presentations that showcase projects or initiatives that led to the win, providing attendees with insider looks at your company's journey. Offering behind-the-scenes tours or demonstrations can further engage guests, making the event memorable. Don't forget that these celebrations are also perfect moments for capturing content – photos, videos, and live streams can be shared across social media and other marketing channels to reach audiences who couldn't attend. Securing sponsorships for these events can reduce costs while expanding network linkages, potentially involving partners whose interests align with yours. Follow up with participants post-event to gather feedback for future improvement and maintain the relationships established during these interactions.

Attracting Clients and Investors Using Awards

For many businesses, winning awards can be a significant milestone. However, the key to leveraging these honors lies in the recognition itself and in how efficiently you utilize them to appeal to potential clients and investors. Awards serve as a credible third-party endorsement that can significantly influence perceptions and decisions. By positioning your award wins strategically, you can convey market leadership—a critical factor in shaping client decisions and boosting investor confidence.

Imagine walking into a meeting room with potential clients already aware of your recent award win. It's an instant conversation starter, even before you begin your sales pitch—the award positions your company as a leader in your industry, which increases credibility. Clients are more likely to trust your expertise, leading to higher chances of closing deals.

Tapping into this perception requires savvy marketing strategies. Tailoring marketing efforts by highlighting relevant awards is essential for engaging specific client segments. For instance, if you've won an innovation award, target tech-savvy or forward-thinking clients who value cutting-edge solutions. Highlighting such achievements in your campaigns helps draw attention from those who share similar values, making your business more relatable and attractive.

Creating guidelines on how to tailor these marketing efforts can provide immense benefits. Start by identifying which awards resonate most with your various client segments. Develop targeted marketing materials that speak directly to their interests. Incorporating testimonials and case studies that link to the prize can further cement your authority and appeal.

Not only do awards capture external interest, but they also offer substantial leverage when integrated into business proposals. In competitive environments, distinguishing your brand is imperative. Including award wins in proposals can set your business apart by demonstrating proven excellence and achievement. This doesn't merely affirm your capabilities; it's a testament to the company's success and industry acknowledgment.

When crafting proposals, consider including detailed descriptions of the awards, criteria for selection, and any related achievements the awards recognize. Such specificity can provide context and underline the importance of the honor beyond its title. Remember, awards should complement your proposal narrative, reinforcing your business strengths.

Building connections is another pivotal area where awards can significantly impact investor relationships. Discussing recent honors during investor meetings can enhance presentations and foster trust. An award signals dedication and accomplishment, qualities investors seek in a prospective partnership. It speaks volumes about your ability to meet and exceed expectations.

To maximize this opportunity, preparing your team with talking points centered around award accomplishments can keep investor meetings focused and impactful. Include anecdotes demonstrating how the award reflects broader organizational goals or strategic directions. This helps build a compelling story around your brand, vividly portraying future growth prospects.

Moreover, awards can act as a bridge in building relationships with investors. They provide a natural segue into conversations about your company's vision and long-term strategy, reinforcing why investing in your company is a wise decision. Awards lend credibility to these discussions and help potential investors envision the potential returns on their investment.

Beyond individual interactions, awards also offer avenues for broader networking opportunities. Being associated with prestigious awards strengthens your visibility in industry circles, attracting like-minded professionals and opening doors to collaborations and partnerships.

Wrapping Up

Throughout this chapter, we've explored how to seamlessly weave award wins into your marketing strategies to boost business growth. For early-stage entrepreneurs and seasoned professionals, awards are potent tools to bolster credibility and visibility. Your brand can stand out in competitive markets by displaying award logos on your marketing materials, sharing successes through engaging advertising and keeping your digital presence updated with your latest achievements. We've also emphasized using compelling narratives in content marketing to share the journey behind your awards. This approach showcases expertise and builds more profound connections with audiences hungry for inspiring success stories.

As we wrap up, consider how these strategies can serve as a blueprint for integrating awards into your broader goals. Whether it's updating your website or leveraging media opportunities, a consistent approach across all channels can amplify the impact of your achievements. Remember, awards offer a unique chance to engage clients and investors while reinforcing trust in your brand's capabilities. With thoughtful implementation, your award wins can be transformed from simple recognitions into powerful catalysts for growth, opening doors to new possibilities and strengthening your position as a leader in your industry.

The upcoming chapter will delve into the art of strategic follow-up after winning awards. How can you keep the momentum going? What follow-up actions turn a single award into a series of opportunities, connections, and collaborations? Prepare to explore the next steps in leveraging your wins to fuel further growth and open doors you may not have thought possible.

10

Strategic Follow-Up After Winning Awards

Winning an award is not just a moment of glory; it's a golden opportunity to propel your career or business forward. Beyond the trophy lies the power to signal a significant achievement that can open doors to continuous growth and fresh possibilities. But how can you make sure it works to your advantage? This chapter will explore strategic ways to use your win as a launchpad for future success. Whether you're an emerging professional eager to strengthen your personal brand or a seasoned business owner aiming to revitalize your reputation, understanding the value of a well-crafted post-award plan is essential. Here, the focus is on transforming your honor into a powerful catalyst that elevates every aspect of your professional journey.

Creating a Post-Award Action Plan

In the world of professional recognition, receiving an award can mark a pivotal moment. Yet, to fully capitalize on this experience for ongoing development, it's essential to formulate a strategic approach that maximizes its advantages. This includes establishing specific goals, identifying practical steps, crafting a detailed timeline, and routinely assessing your progress.

To effectively harness the benefits of an award, the initial task is to define clear goals. Awards naturally increase visibility and credibility, making it crucial to connect these outcomes with personal or organizational ambitions. For emerging professionals and aspiring entrepreneurs, this might entail utilizing the award to solidify their personal brand. In contrast, seasoned business owners may aim to revitalize their brand image among industry colleagues. Clear goals enable you to utilize the award as a launching pad for greater success, whether it involves expanding your professional network, increasing client inquiries, or enhancing your market presence.

Once the goals are established, it's imperative to pinpoint targeted actions that turn these objectives into reality. Start by updating your website to showcase your new accolade prominently. A well-prepared press release can disseminate your achievement to a broader audience, drawing potential media interest and fresh opportunities. Additionally, create promotional materials like brochures or social media content that spotlight the award, broadening your message across various platforms. Including testimonials or case studies tied to the honor can further enhance your credibility.

A helpful principle to adhere to is ensuring that each action supports the overall narrative of your brand identity. This unity aids in delivering a coherent story to your audience and stakeholders. Integrating these actions with your existing mission reinforces your brand's fundamental values and facilitates the smooth inclusion of the award into your ongoing narrative.

Establishing a timeline is crucial for effectively managing these initiatives. A well-structured schedule guarantees that each task is accomplished promptly, optimizing the momentum gained from the award. Begin with short-term objectives like initial promotional ventures and gradually transition to long-term strategies, such as forging partnerships or launching new projects that take advantage of your enhanced profile. Define milestones to monitor progress and make necessary adjustments if obstacles or delays occur. The timeline acts as a guide, leading you through each stage while keeping the overarching goals in focus.

To ensure continued success, regularly review and refine your strategy. Strategic planning is dynamic; it demands flexibility and the ability to adapt to changing circumstances. Assess whether the actions you've executed are achieving your set goals. Are you observing an increase in website visitors? Are fresh clients approaching due to your award-promoted initiatives? Utilize key metrics to evaluate your effectiveness quantitatively. If specific methods aren't yielding the expected results, be prepared to adjust. This may involve modifying your marketing strategy or discovering new avenues for engagement.

Cultivating a culture of ongoing enhancement is essential. As you gather data and insights from your efforts, use them to shape future tactics, maintaining a proactive and progressive stance. This iterative process fortifies your brand and positions you favorably for new opportunities.

Engaging your team in the strategic planning process boosts involvement and fosters a sense of ownership. Motivate team members to share ideas and provide feedback, ensuring everyone is committed to the collective objectives. Teamwork often leads to innovative solutions and aids in comprehensive execution aligned across all organizational levels. Delineate responsibilities so each individual understands their role in the strategy. This division of tasks encourages accountability and keeps the entire team focused on achieving shared goals.

Tracking Metrics for Long-Term Impact

Monitoring and measuring an award's effects over time is essential to harness its value and propel your growth. Every honor has a potential ripple effect that can enhance your brand's visibility, credibility, and interest. By systematically examining these impacts, you can ensure your award continues to serve your endeavors well after the initial celebration.

Begin with identifying key metrics that signify the reach and influence of your award recognition. These include website traffic patterns, the number of business inquiries, social media engagement, or even a surge in direct sales. Though it might be tempting to track everything, focus on those indicators most relevant to your strategic goals. For instance, if increasing the digital footprint was a primary aim, then shifts in website visits and online interactions would become especially pertinent metrics to watch.

Next, creating a robust tracking system is indispensable. Implement tools such as Google Analytics or specialized software to gather detailed data from your platforms. Establishing baseline figures before your award announcement allows you to gauge apparent changes post-recognition accurately. It's not just about observing metrics but understanding them in the context of your broader objectives. Interpreting data correctly can reveal significant trends: your award has doubled website visitors from a specific demographic, indicating newfound opportunities in untapped markets.

Analyzing the collected data involves more than crunching numbers; it's about deriving insights that inform future actions. Look for patterns that suggest what's resonating with your audience. Have certain content pieces seen heightened engagement since your award? It could hint at consumer preferences worth noting for future campaigns. Similarly, if business inquiries have surged while conversion rates remain steady, it may indicate a need to refine your sales approach or enhance the customer experience on your website.

As you delve deeper into these insights, adapt and refine

your strategies accordingly. Awards can open doors to new avenues—you might discover niche audiences or potential partnerships previously unexplored. Consistently reviewing and reevaluating data helps you stay adaptable and responsive to changing market conditions.

Transparency is another critical component of maximizing ROI from awards. Craft comprehensive reports summarizing your findings and accomplishments, ready to share with stakeholders. These reports are powerful tools for illustrating tangible returns on investment from your accolades. When communicating these outcomes, focus on clarity and simplicity. Highlight significant achievements, such as notable increases in engagement metrics or successful conversions attributable to the award, using visuals like charts or graphs for added impact.

These insights benefit stakeholders—including team members, investors, and partners—and encourage a culture of collaboration and shared vision. They offer reassurance that your efforts are driving value while potentially inspiring further support and investment in your initiatives. Transparency builds trust, reinforcing the narrative that your brand is continuously evolving and capitalizing on its successes.

Implementing guidelines strategically can streamline these processes, ensuring consistency and efficiency. For example, create a standard procedure for gathering and analyzing data post-award, defining specific roles and timelines to avoid bottlenecks. Clear report generation and dissemination checkpoints can prevent miscommunication and ensure relevant stakeholders receive timely updates. By embedding these practices into your operations, you maintain momentum and keep your award's positive influence alive long-term.

Engaging with Award Sponsors and Judges

Strategic follow-up after winning an award can be crucial in capitalizing on the success and ensuring continuous growth. One of the most effective strategies is building relationships and networking for future opportunities. This process begins with reaching out to those involved in your award path, such as sponsors or judges, by sending personalized thank-you notes. Not only do these messages express gratitude, but they also serve as the starting point for meaningful connections that may lead to future collaborations. By acknowledging their role in your achievement, you create a foundation of goodwill that can be leveraged for new partnerships and ventures.

When drafting these notes, it's essential to be genuine. People can often tell if someone is merely seeking personal gain, so sincerity is critical. Focus on what you appreciated about their support or feedback and how it impacted your journey. This approach not only shows gratitude but also reinforces mutual respect, paving the way for more substantive interactions down the line. For example, if a judge provided valuable insights during the competition, mention how their advice helped refine your approach.

Next, consider attending industry events hosted by these sponsors or judges. Such gatherings offer unparalleled opportunities to augment your brand presence within influential circles. When preparing to participate, research the event thoroughly and plan which individuals or groups you'd like to connect with. Bring business cards and have your elevator pitch ready. Remember, engagement is vital—don't just attend; actively participate. Ask questions during panels, contribute to discussions, and, most importantly, network during breaks or social hours.

These events are treasure troves for expanding your professional circle. By interacting with peers, industry leaders, and potential collaborators, you showcase your achievements and establish yourself as a proactive and involved member of your community. During these interactions, focus on listening just as much as talking. Show genuine interest in others' work and ask thoughtful questions. This exchange of ideas can foster deeper connections and lead to future collaborative projects.

Another strategic approach is to keep your sponsors and judges updated about your progress post-award. Regular communication helps maintain the relationship and demonstrates the ongoing impact of your recognition. Thanks to their support, it's helpful to share milestones or successes that have occurred. This sharing shows that their involvement continues to bear fruit and keeps you top-of-mind should any new opportunities arise.

Consider sending quarterly updates via email or posting achievements on professional networks like LinkedIn. Highlight concrete accomplishments from the initial award recognition, such as new projects or expansions. Being open and honest builds connections and encourages ongoing guidance and teamwork. (Nwankwo, 2024)

Lastly, pay attention to the power of seeking mentorship from those judges and sponsors who have supported your career. Mentors can provide invaluable insights into industry trends, challenges, and emerging opportunities that might take time to become apparent. To identify a mentor, you must recognize individuals whose careers or expertise align with your goals. Don't hesitate to reach out and express your desire to learn from their experiences. Be clear about why you're seeking their guidance and what you hope to achieve.

Mentorships thrive on mutual respect and open communication. Set clear expectations and maintain regular contact through periodic meetings or informal catch-ups. In return, find ways to offer value—perhaps by assisting them with a project or sharing your insights. This reciprocal relationship can significantly boost your career trajectory, providing advice and encouragement when navigating complex decisions.

These strategies are particularly relevant for young professionals and aspiring entrepreneurs. Building a robust network and maintaining these relationships can significantly boost personal brand credibility and visibility. Leveraging award wins as a stepping stone to creating lasting industry relationships can set the stage for sustained success in one's field.

Meanwhile, established professionals looking to refresh their brand must also see the value in such strategic engagements. Awards can reinvigorate a reputation, positioning individuals as thought leaders or innovators. Engaging with past judges and sponsors shows adaptability and forward-thinking, essential for maintaining authority in ever-evolving industries.

Lessons Learned

This chapter discussed the importance of creating a solid plan after receiving an award. We found that to make the most of an award for growth, it's vital to set clear goals and take focused actions. Whether you're a new professional building your image or a business owner wanting to improve your reputation, linking your goals to your achievements can lead to greater success. Every step, from updating your online profile to connecting with the media and influential people, should reflect your brand's main message, ensuring you stay consistent and genuine. Making a timeline helps you stay organized, while regularly checking your progress with essential measures allows your plan to change as needed.

Engagement with award sponsors and judges opens doors to new opportunities and connections. You can strengthen networks that support growth by expressing genuine gratitude and seeking mentorship. Attending relevant events and staying in contact with these key figures enhances relationships and amplifies your industry presence. As you progress, remember that when used wisely, awards can unlock new possibilities for the future. Through strategic planning and meaningful interactions, your award can catalyze long-term achievement and sustained impact in your professional realm.

11

Continuous Growth Beyond Awards

What if winning an award was your success story's beginning rather than the end? Imagine using every win—or even every near miss—as a stepping stone toward becoming a recognized expert and a continuously evolving professional. Award experiences, often seen as the pinnacle of achievement, can offer much more than a moment of recognition. They present a unique opportunity for introspection and growth that goes beyond the shining moment on stage. By examining our triumphs and missteps in award applications, individuals can uncover invaluable insights into their personal and professional careers. This reflection opens doors to understanding what truly matters in their craft and how they wish to evolve further.

In this chapter, readers are invited to explore how these experiences can become powerful catalysts for their ongoing development. The thrill of winning might diminish over time, but the lessons gleaned from these moments have a lasting impact. They guide us toward refining skills, embracing constructive feedback, and setting new benchmarks for success.

By crafting structured action plans and tracking growth through innovative tools, individuals can ensure that progress remains aligned with broader objectives. The exploration doesn't stop at self-reflection; this chapter encourages you to venture into new skill areas and seek opportunities that challenge the status quo. Maintaining a forward-looking perspective makes the path to sustained achievement more evident, empowering professionals to enhance their brand and influence continuously in an ever-evolving landscape.

Evaluating Past Performances for Insights

Reflecting on past award experiences can be valuable, especially when striving for continuous growth. To begin with, understanding how to analyze previous applications effectively is essential. This process involves diving into each aspect of your submission to recognize what worked well and what didn't. One reflection technique is to create a simple checklist of questions: Which sections of your application stood out? Were there parts that needed more clarity or detail? By systematically reviewing these elements, you can start to identify patterns. Perhaps you consistently excel in articulating your vision but falter in providing statistical evidence to support your claims. Recognizing such strengths and weaknesses allows for targeted improvement.

Integrating feedback from judges or mentors is equally important in this growth process. Feedback provides an external perspective that can illuminate blind spots we might overlook. Judges often offer specific comments on your application—these are golden nuggets of wisdom waiting to be mined. A judge's note about being "too vague" in certain sections offers a clear directive for future applications. Similarly, mentors can guide you by sharing their insights and experiences, helping you refine your approach. Engaging in a mindset that embraces constructive rather than critical feedback is important. Consider setting up regular sessions with a mentor to review feedback comprehensively, allowing you to make continuous improvements.

Defining success metrics is another fundamental strategy for ongoing personal and professional advancement. Success, particularly in the context of awards, often centers around recognition and achievement. However, actual growth stems from establishing personalized metrics that transcend just winning an accolade. Start by outlining what success means to you beyond the award. Is it increased visibility in your industry, the opportunity to network with peers, or personal satisfaction derived from honing a particular skill? Once you've defined these metrics, set measurable goals linked to them. For example, if networking is a success metric, aim to connect with at least three new professionals per event. Monitoring these goals ensures that your progress aligns with your broader objectives, creating a path beyond mere recognition.

Creating structured action plans is instrumental in translating reflections and feedback into tangible results. An action plan acts as a roadmap, guiding you through clearly defined steps toward future success. Start by pinpointing one or two areas identified during your reflection and feedback process that need development. Next, break down larger goals into smaller, manageable tasks with specific deadlines. For instance, if enhancing the narrative portion of your application is a priority, allocate time weekly to practice storytelling techniques or enroll in a relevant workshop. Document these steps in a dedicated journal or digital file, regularly updating it to reflect progress and adjust strategies as needed. Establishing accountability partners can also bolster this process. Sharing your goals and progress with someone trusted can motivate you to stay committed and provide further insights.

Implementing dashboards or run charts, as used in performance evaluations (Agency for Healthcare Research and Quality, 2020), could be adapted for tracking personal growth metrics. These tools allow you to visually map progress over time, making it easier to assess whether you're moving toward your defined success metrics. By charting milestones against timelines, you better understand your trajectory and areas requiring attention.

Exploring New Areas for Development

In the quest for continuous growth beyond awards, seeking new skills and knowledge areas is indispensable. Awards can provide recognition, but they should be seen as stepping stones rather than destinations. By seeking holistic development, individuals can guarantee long-term personal and professional success.

Identifying skill gaps is the first step towards this holistic development. Understanding where one's abilities fall short compared to one's aspirations helps set clear learning targets. Frameworks for assessing these skill gaps can guide individuals toward identifying pertinent areas for improvement. Start by evaluating your current competencies and your future goals. Ask yourself: What skills do I need to reach my next career milestone? Which areas of knowledge could augment my performance or open new opportunities? Conducting a self-assessment or utilizing tools like 360-degree feedback can provide insights into these gaps, offering a roadmap for further development.

Once skill gaps are identified, the next step is finding appropriate learning opportunities. Many options are available today, catering to different learning styles and needs. Workshops, for example, offer hands-on experience and can be an excellent choice for practical skills training. They provide immediate feedback and foster an interactive learning environment. Courses offer flexibility and access to expert knowledge worldwide, particularly online ones. Whether enrolling in a university course or a certification program, selecting ones that align with your long-term objectives is vital. Additionally, attending conferences can expose you to industry trends, thought leaders, and potential collaborators. These events are learning opportunities and platforms to expand your network, which can be instrumental in discovering new development paths.

CONTINUOUS GROWTH BEYOND AWARDS

Networking is often undervalued when it comes to personal growth. However, building meaningful connections in your industry can reveal hidden opportunities for skill development. Engaging with professionals who have diverse experiences can offer fresh perspectives and advice. One powerful strategy is to join relevant industry groups or associations, which can provide access to mentorship programs or exclusive training sessions. Participate actively in discussions, whether on social media forums or at relationship-building events, as these interactions can lead to collaborations and partnerships that nurture growth. Remember, every connection has the potential to unveil a new avenue for learning and advancement.

Embracing a trial-and-error approach in skill development is necessary. Not everything will go perfectly the first time, and that's okay. Experimenting with new methods, applying different strategies, and occasionally encountering failure can be some of the most valuable learning experiences. Developing a mindset that views setbacks as opportunities for growth is essential to continual progress.

I highly recommend *Failing Forward*, an inspiring book by one of my mentors, Dr. John C. Maxwell. In this work, Dr. Maxwell explores the idea that failure is not the opposite of success but a crucial part of it. Reframing failures as stepping stones toward growth, he encourages readers to embrace resilience and adaptability—essential qualities in today's ever-evolving professional world.

For example, if you're interested in digital marketing, consider a small-scale project, like managing social media for a friend's business. This hands-on experience allows you to apply theoretical knowledge in real-world scenarios, helping you refine your skills organically over time. Remember, the path of skill acquisition is rarely linear; instead, it's about persistence, flexibility, and a commitment to learning from each experience.

Throughout this journey, it's essential to remain open to feedback and adjust your strategies accordingly. By incorporating constructive criticism, you can fine-tune your approach to learning and development. Measuring your progress against set goals ensures you are moving in the right direction. Celebrate the milestones and use them as motivation to continue pushing boundaries.

Remember, pursuing new skills and knowledge isn't a one-time effort; it's an ongoing process. Just as industries evolve, so too must your capabilities. Stay curious and motivated to learn and explore various subjects outside your immediate field, as interdisciplinary knowledge can drive innovation and creativity. A well-rounded skill set will empower you to leverage award experiences as more than just recognition—it will make them catalysts for sustained growth and achievement in your career.

Staying Updated on Industry Trends

In an era of rapid transformation, keeping up with industry changes is essential for personal and professional advancement. The prestige and acknowledgment associated with industry awards represent a significant achievement for many individuals. However, beyond these honors, how can one consistently thrive in an ever-shifting environment? The solution lies in utilizing trend analysis techniques—practical tools that keep you updated on advancements in your sector and assist you in responding to changes adeptly.

Trend analysis investigates existing patterns to forecast future developments, providing crucial insights into market needs or technological progress. Techniques like SWOT analysis (evaluating strengths, weaknesses, opportunities, and threats) and PEST analysis (analyzing political, economic, social, and technological factors) prove especially beneficial. By routinely employing these techniques, you can recognize potential shifts in consumer preferences or breakthrough technologies that may redefine the industry. This proactive strategy helps you remain relevant and places you in a strong position as new award categories or criteria emerge.

Industry trends frequently correspond with opportunities and expectations for awards. Take, for instance, the rising domains of artificial intelligence and renewable energy. As these industries grow, associated awards emphasize innovation, sustainability, and ethical standards. Keeping abreast of such trends allows you to synchronize your efforts with the evolving expectations of award-giving organizations, enhancing your likelihood of recognition. Grasping the trajectory of your sector enables you to predict what evaluators will appreciate in future nomination rounds.

To maintain competitiveness, it's vital to refine your practices to correspond with evolving trends continuously. This might involve integrating advanced technologies, embracing more sustainable operational methods, or creating innovative products and services that resonate with contemporary market demands. For example, if data analytics is increasingly becoming critical in your area, consider enhancing your skills in this discipline or investing in relevant analytics tools. Remaining nimble ensures that your initiatives are consistent with industry directions, positioning you as a frontrunner for accolades celebrating innovative contributions.

Beyond immediate professional benefits, utilizing industry trends to shape and enhance your personal brand is a strategic choice that yields long-term rewards. A robust personal brand is characterized by authenticity, expertise, and uniqueness—all attributes that can be enriched through trend engagement. When your endeavors consistently reflect the latest industry movements, they boost your credibility and amplify your influence in your professional circle. For instance, frequently sharing insights on trending topics through blogs, webinars, or social media establishes you as a thought leader.

Developing a compelling personal brand that mirrors ongoing trends necessitates several tactical approaches. Begin by evaluating how your skills and experiences mesh with industry shifts. Are you an experienced professional with a deep understanding of emerging markets or a pioneer in introducing innovative concepts to traditional practices? Catalog these strengths and communicate them effectively across your digital presence. Platforms such as LinkedIn, Instagram, X (formerly Twitter), and your personal website are vital for crafting a unified brand that reflects your career ambitions and expertise.

Active participation in your professional community further reinforces your branding efforts. Engage in conversations on trending subjects, publish insightful articles, and collaborate with colleagues who share your interests. These interactions broaden your perspective and affirm your position as a knowledgeable contributor. Importantly, these engagements should come across as genuine, enhancing the credibility of your personal brand.

Multimedia presents additional opportunities to enrich your brand narrative. Videos, podcasts, and infographics cater to diverse audiences and simplify complex concepts. Harnessing these formats can significantly expand your reach and appeal. Imagine launching a podcast series that delves into recent advancements in your field or creating a video tutorial that simplifies a trending technology. These creative projects showcase your adaptability and willingness to utilize new platforms, traits that are highly valued in award considerations.

Ultimately, while consistency in presenting your personal brand is crucial, the ability to evolve is equally important. Regularly assessing your online identity ensures its relevance amid industry changes. Solicit peer input to understand how your brand is perceived and adjust your messaging as necessary. This iterative approach prevents stagnation and ensures you remain prominent as trends shift.

Final Thoughts

Looking back on the ideas in this chapter, it's clear that using award experiences can help your career grow. By thinking about what you've done in the past, asking important questions, and getting feedback from judges and mentors, you build a strong base for improvement and ongoing success. Achieving goals isn't just about winning awards; it's about setting personal goals and making plans that align with your giant dreams. Whether improving your storytelling, making new connections, or gaining more knowledge in your field, each action keeps you moving forward, ensuring that every award helps you grow in your career.

Also, learning new skills and gaining insights can turn awards from just a finish line into tools for long-term growth. By finding areas where you can improve and looking for chances to learn, you can develop well-rounded. Networking helps you discover new ideas and build partnerships. Staying aware of what's happening in your industry ensures you remain competitive and keep growing. This journey is about constant learning and adapting, where every award helps you reach bigger goals.

But with this momentum, a question remains: How do you combine all these threads of growth, recognition, and strategy into a cohesive, lasting impact? As we move into the final section, we'll explore how to shape these experiences into a powerful, enduring legacy that defines your professional brand and vision.

12

Conclusion

As we come to the end of our exploration into the transformative power of awards, we must pause and reflect on the journey we've taken together. This book has guided you through the dynamic landscape where personal ambition meets professional recognition. Whether you're a young professional eager to carve out your niche or an established business owner looking to strengthen your brand, pursuing awards is more than just a quest for accolades; it's a fundamental tool for growth and development.

Throughout these pages, we've delved into how awards catalyze personal and business transformation. We've explored how they offer a platform to showcase your skills and achievements and reshape your narrative in your industry. Each award application you complete isn't merely about adding another trophy to your shelf; it's an opportunity to refine and enhance your personal brand and elevate your professional credibility. The stories shared in this book have shown us that this experience can change how you perceive yourself and others—a stepping stone towards unparalleled opportunities.

This transformative experience isn't something you undertake alone. One of our discussions' most powerful insights has been the community's incredible role in this process. The power of networking and support cannot be overstated. Surrounding yourself with like-minded individuals who share your ambitions helps cultivate a support system that drives you forward and enriches the rewards of the path you take. Connecting with peers turns challenges into manageable tasks and victories into meaningful celebrations.

Now, as we stand at this juncture, it's time to take all the insights you've gained and translate them into action. Armed with strategies and practical advice, you can make significant strides toward your goals. Remember, success is born from action. Every tip and piece of wisdom shared here is a stepping stone for creating your own path to success. As one aspiring entrepreneur vividly expressed, implementing these tips instilled a sense of control over their career trajectory, making them feel empowered like never before.

In addition to action, fostering a growth mindset is equally important. The game doesn't end with applying for awards—it involves continuous learning and self-improvement. Every application and every outcome, whether expected or surprising, is a learning opportunity. Embrace each step, each triumph, and each setback as part of your growth process. As one past award winner wisely stated, seeing challenges as lessons helped fuel growth far beyond any tangible reward could provide. This resilience and willingness to adapt and learn propels

CONCLUSION

individuals to new heights.

Looking towards the future, it's essential to envision how ongoing recognition can impact your career and life in lasting ways. Picture your future self, enriched by the experiences and recognitions along this path. Consider the doors that will open, the networks that will expand, and the opportunities that will arise because of your endeavors. Recognition isn't a moment of glory but a springboard for more significant achievements. One recent recipient noted that winning an award wasn't just a moment of pride—it was the catalyst for their next big venture, setting the stage for even more ambitious projects.

As you contemplate your next steps post-reading, carry with you the understanding that awards indeed hold the potential to transform your professional career. They're more than metallic statues; they're potent narratives of your ability, perseverance, and vision. Think about how you can leverage this knowledge to create lasting impacts on your career. Continue to seek recognition not as an endpoint but as a launchpad for what lies ahead.

The trajectory towards recognition and credibility is ongoing, evolving with each endeavor you undertake. Remember to keep pushing forward and be open to learning, connecting, and growing. Each application, each connection, and each recognition is a chapter in your professional story, one that speaks to your commitment to excellence and your desire to make a meaningful impact on the world around you. Embrace the tools and strategies discussed throughout this book and let them guide you as you forge forward with confidence and clarity.

In conclusion, consider this book your companion on the exciting journey of building your personal and professional legacy through awards. While the path may present challenges, it's precisely within these trials that your true character and potential emerge. Pursuing awards is about more than recognition; it's about becoming the person capable of achieving greatness. Armed with the knowledge and inspiration you've gained, set forth on this path with renewed purpose and determination. Your journey of recognition and success begins now—take the next step and make it happen!

References

afshinkalhori@admin. (2024, October 20). *Mind Tips for Better Mental Health: Boost Your Wellbeing Today*. Parcian Mag. https://parcian.com/mag/mind-tips-for-better-mental-health/

Agency for Healthcare Research and Quality. (2020, January). *Section 4: Ways to approach the quality improvement process*. Agency for Healthcare Research and Quality. https://www.ahrq.gov/cahps/quality-improvement/improvement-guide/4-approach-qi-process/index.html

Aldridge, E. (2024, June 28). *Identify Skills Gaps and Training Needs for Optimal Growth*. Educate 360 Professional Training Partners. https://educate360.com/blog/identifying-skil-gaps-and-training-needs/

Author, B. (2021, October 25). *Why Attending Networking Events Is Beneficial For Your Business*. www.baass.com. https://www.baass.com/blog/why-attending-networking-events-is-beneficial-for-your-business

Avery, J., & Greenwald, R. (2023, May). *A New Approach to Building Your Personal Brand*. Harvard Business Review. https://hbr.org/2023/05/a-new-approach-to-building-you

r-personal-brand

Bay. (2024, July 15). *Best Self-Improvement Activities to Transform Your Life*. Bay Area CBT Center. https://bayareacbtcenter.com/self-improvement-activities/

Bi Worldwide. (2023, October 30). *How do Rewards Impact Employee Performance?* BI WORLDWIDE. https://www.biworldwide.co.uk/biworldwide-research-materials/blog/employee-engagement/how-do-rewards-impact-employee-performance/

Bravata, D. M., Watts, S. A., Keefer, A. L., Madhusudhan, D. K., Taylor, K. T., Clark, D. M., Nelson, R. S., Cokley, K. O., & Hagg, H. K. (2019, December 17). *Prevalence, Predictors, and Treatment of Impostor Syndrome: a Systematic Review*. Journal of General Internal Medicine. https://doi.org/10.1007/s11606-019-05364-1

Chauhan, T. (2023, April 5). *Why Awards Matter: Reflections on External Validation and Intrinsic Motivation*. Medium; The Side Hustle Club. https://medium.com/the-side-hustle-club/why-awards-matter-reflections-on-external-validation-and-intrinsic-motivation-f8f25b52d3d2

Cote, C. (2024, March 21). *Personal Branding: What It Is and Why It Matters*. Business Insights Blog. https://online.hbs.edu/blog/post/personal-branding-at-work

Eastman, M. (2010, February 18). *Malcolm Baldrige National Quality Award*. NIST. https://www.nist.gov/baldrige/baldrige-

REFERENCES

award

Editor-2 Editor-2. (2023, November 4). *SWOT Analysis: Best Practices, Templates, and Examples.* Holistique Training. https://www.holistiquetraining.com/en/news/what-is-the-meaning-of-swot-analysis

Effective Storytelling Techniques - FasterCapital. (2024). *Effective Storytelling Techniques - FasterCapital.* FasterCapital. https://fastercapital.com/topics/effective-storytelling-techniques.html

15 SMART Leadership Goals Examples to Inspire and Motivate Growth. (2024). Deel.com. https://www.deel.com/blog/smart-leadership-goals-examples/
Forttuna Global Excellence Awards. (2024). Forttuna.co. https://forttuna.co/healthcare-award/

Fresen, N. (2024, February 13). *The Impact of Employee Awards on Retail Company Culture - The People In Retail Awards.* The People in Retail Awards. https://peopleinretailawards.com/impact-of-employee-awards-on-retail-company-culture/

Fusman, A. (n.d.). *Council Post: Win Awards To Differentiate Your Brand, Build Loyalty And Sell More.* Forbes. https://www.forbes.com/sites/forbescommunicationscouncil/2017/08/08/win-awards-to-differentiate-your-brand-build-loyalty-and-sell-more/

Gallup. (2016, June 28). *Employee Recognition: Low Cost, High Impact.* Gallup. https://www.gallup.com/workplace/236441/

employee-recognition-low-cost-high-impact.aspx

Globee Awards. (2023, July 25). *Crafting a Legacy: How Awards Shape Your Career Path and Leave a Lasting Impact.* Globee® Business Awards. https://globeeawards.com/crafting-a-legacy-how-awards-shape-your-career-path-and-leave-a-lasting-impact/

Gorbatov, S., Khapova, S. N., & Lysova, E. I. (2018). *Personal branding: Interdisciplinary systematic review and research agenda. Frontiers in Psychology,* 9, Article 2238. https://doi.org/10.3389/fpsyg.2018.02238

Harrison, B., & Jepsen, D. M. (2015, August). *The career impact of winning an external work-related award.* Journal of Vocational Behavior. https://doi.org/10.1016/j.jvb.2015.04.004

Hebert, M. (2023, July 21). *Tips Behind the Art of Being an Accountability Partner.* TopResume; Tips Behind the Art of Being an Accountability Partner | TopResume. https://ca.topresume.com/career-advice/tips-behind-the-art-of-being-an-accountability-partner

Hofmann, A. (2023, April 14). *How To Effectively Communicate Your Strategic Plan To Employees | ClearPoint Strategy.* www.clearpointstrategy.com. https://www.clearpointstrategy.com/blog/communicating-strategy-be-effective

How Employee Recognition Impacts Business Initiatives at Large Companies. (n.d.). Www.octanner.com. https://www.octanner.

REFERENCES

com/articles/business-impact-of-recognition

How To Grow Website Traffic? Sources, Tactics, Tips & More. (n.d.). Website. https://vwo.com/grow-website-traffic/

Huecker, M. R., Shreffler, J., McKeny, P. T., & Davis, D. (2023, July 31). *Imposter Phenomenon.* PubMed; StatPearls Publishing. https://www.ncbi.nlm.nih.gov/books/NBK585058/

Jobya. (2024, May). *Navigating Workplace Challenges: The Impact of Social Media on Professional Relationships.* Jobya. https://jobya.com/learn/workplace/navigating_workplace_challenges/the_impact_of_social_media_on_professional_relationships

Judging Process. (2024, October 20). Globee® Business Awards. https://globeeawards.com/judging-and-awards-process/

Karpenkova, A. (2023, July 3). *How to Identify Training Gaps (+Overcoming Them) | Whatfix.* The Whatfix Blog | Drive Digital Adoption. https://whatfix.com/blog/identify-training-gaps/

Knight, R. (2024, May 16). *Your Social Media Presence Can Help You Land (or Lose) a Job Opportunity.* Harvard Business Review. https://hbr.org/2024/05/your-social-media-presence-can-help-you-land-or-lose-a-job-opportunity

lifecoachtraining. (2023, July 12). *Understanding the Psychology of Motivation in Goal Setting.* Life Coach Certification Online. https://lifecoachtraining.co/understanding-the-psychology-of-motivation-in-goal-setting/

Manage Stress and Prioritize Mental Health: Techniques for Well-being in a Fast-Paced World. (2024). Wellcarecommunityhealth.org. https://www.wellcarecommunityhealth.org/education/manage-stress-and-prioritize-mental-health-techniques-for-well-being-in-a-fast-paced-world

Marketing Strategy: Best practices for awards. (2024). Haveignition.com. https://www.haveignition.com/best-practices/marketing-strategy-best-practices-for-awards

Matejko, S. (2022, February 9). *Marketing Awards Guidebook: Why It Matters, What To Enter And How To Win*. Forbes. https://www.forbes.com/sites/forbescontentmarketing/2022/02/09/marketing-awards-guidebook-why-it-matters-what-to-enter-and-how-to-win/

Michael Page. (2022). *Top 12 Benefits Of Networking: Why Networking Is Important*. Michael Page. https://www.michaelpage.com.au/advice/career-advice/career-progression/top-12-benefits-networking-why-networking-important

Morrison, Courtney. (2021, March 9). *10 Personal Brand Statement Examples for Inspiration*. EveryoneSocial. https://everyonesocial.com/blog/personal-brand-statement-examples/

Networking and relationship building for career success. (2023, November 27). Marquette. https://online.marquette.edu/business/blog/networking-and-relationship-building-for-career-success

News, T. P. (2024). *The PIEoneer Awards 2024*. Pieoneer-

REFERENCES

awards.com. https://pieoneerawards.com/2024/en/page/categories-

Nwankwo, E. C. (2024, July 25). *The Importance of Networking: How to Build Valuable Connections.* Medium. https://ericnwankwo.medium.com/the-importance-of-networking-how-to-build-valuable-connections-16103d982f3e

O'Flaherty, S., Sanders, M. T., & Whillans, A. (2021, March 29). *Research: A Little Recognition Can Provide a Big Morale Boost.* Harvard Business Review. https://hbr.org/2021/03/research-a-little-recognition-can-provide-a-big-morale-boost

Processes and Procedures: Strategies for How to Effectively Implement in Your Business Flowster. (2023, July 14). https://flowster.app/processes-and-procedures-implementation-strategies/

Radulovski, A. (2024, March 20). *What Are the Key Benefits of Mentorship for Women Starting Their Own Businesses?* Women in Tech Network. https://www.womentech.net/how-to/what-are-key-benefits-mentorship-women-starting-their-own-businesses

Rhythmq. (2023, October 20). *Streamlining Awards Judging with Award Management Software.* RQ Platform. https://rqawards.com/streamlining-awards-judging-with-award-management-software/

Saxena, T. (2023, November 18). *How to Overcome Self-Rejection and Move into Self-Acceptance?* Medium. https://tinasaxena.medium.com/how-to-overcome-self-rejection-and-move-into-s

elf-acceptance-83a2c82d6ca9

7 Ways To Effectively Reframe Rejection. (2023, November 7). Brook. https://www.brook.org.uk/blog/7-ways-to-effectively-reframe-rejection/

Social Media & Digital Awards 2024. (2024, February 5). PR Daily. https://www.prdaily.com/awards/social-media-digital-awards/2024/

Stephenson, S. (2021, July 29). *Measuring the Success of Social Media Campaigns.* LOCALiQ. https://localiq.co.uk/blog/how-to-measure-the-success-of-a-social-media-campaign

Team, M. (2024, March 14). *Exploring the benefits of employee recognition programs: Strategies and impacts.* https://www.mavenclinic.com. https://www.mavenclinic.com/post/exploring-the-benefits-of-employee-recognition-programs-strategies-and-impacts

The Ultimate Guide to Goal Setting | DailyBot Insights. (2024). Dailybot.com. https://www.dailybot.com/insights/the-ultimate-guide-to-goal-setting

TRH. (2024, April). *Empowering Caregivers: Practical Stress Management.* Therapyrelief.com. https://www.therapyrelief.com/empowering-caregivers-practical-stress-management-techniques/

2025 Digital Awards. (2024, May 29). PRNEWS. https://www.prnewsonline.com/go/2025-digital-awards/

REFERENCES

Twine. (2022, October 18). *Personal SWOT Analysis: Quick Guide & Examples | Twine.* Twine Blog. https://www.twine.net/blog/personal-swot-analysi/

Walker-Ford, M., & Walker-Ford, M. (2018, October 28). *The Science of Storytelling: How Your Business Can Take Advantage - Infographic.* Red Website Design. https://red-website-design.co.uk/storytelling-science-infographic/

Wickham, N. (2023, July 6). *The Importance of Employee Recognition: Statistics and Research.* Quantum Workplace. https://www.quantumworkplace.com/future-of-work/importance-of-employee-recognition

Women of Influence. (2024, April 23). *Personal Branding in the Digital Age: Five Strategic Approaches to...* Women of Influence. https://www.womenofinfluence.ca/2024/04/23/personal-branding-in-the-digital-age-five-strategic-approaches-to-elevate-your-online-presence-and-influence/

Wright, T. (2023, May 3). *The 6-Step Guide to Strategy Implementation.* Www.cascade.app. https://www.cascade.app/blog/guide-to-strategy-implementation

www.ingramcontent.com/pod-product-compliance
Lightning Source LLC
Chambersburg PA
CBHW050305230526
45471CB00005B/2035